Mountain Devotional

...He went up apart to pray

By

Candy Beebe and Julie A R Stephens

This book is dedicated to all those seeking happiness and the purpose of life.

Special thanks to our brilliant editors: Susie Wheaton and Erin Cavit, also such loving friends.

Mountain Devotional
© Copyright, 2013, 2023
by Julie Stephens and Candy Beebe
All rights reserved.
Hands Be Strong, Inc.
handsbestrong.com

No part of this book may be used or reproduced in any manner whatsoever without written permission, except in the case of brief quotations embodied in critical articles or reviews.

9 8 7 6 5 4 3

First Edition August 2013
Third Printing March 2023

ISBN: 978-0-9742680-7-1 (print)
ISBN: 978-0-9742680-8-8 (eBook)

Library of Congress Control Number: 2013941317

Reviews of **Mountain Devotional**

"I got chills reading this devotional. Candy and Julie have reminded me why I live here, and that the good book provides the answers to questions we may have."

> Bernadette Hagendorf, Lake City, Colorado resident and current St. James Episcopal Church representative for the Lake City, Youth Council

"Let the authors gracefully take you on a breathtaking journey, savoring the painted beauty of God's arresting, stately creation. Be forewarned. They take you a bit further than you might expect, pulling back the curtain of creation itself. Behind it shines the blinding light of its Regal Architect, radiating His brilliant power, beauty, and intimate compassion. People who have seen such things seldom remain unchanged."

> David Booth, PhD, is the Minister of Education and Family Discipleship at First Baptist Church in Winnsboro, Texas. David and his wife Christy have three children

"I have been reading around in the writings of Thomas Berry recently and your book affirms his contention that nature is the primary source of revelation. It was here, eons ago, long before the Scriptures were written for us as revelation and displays, magnificently the majestic presence of God in all he has created, the great and the small."

> The Rev. John Manahan retired Catholic Priest, former high school teacher

"Many people come to the Rocky Mountains for various reasons. Now, with this wonderful book, the glory, beauty, and majesty of God's creation in the San Juan Range of the Rocky Mountains can come to you wherever you live. As most of these devotions begins and ends with pertinent Bible verses, this devotional is a variety of thoughts, ideas, and inspirations derived from life in the Rocky Mountains. Many of us who live in the Rockies, including I am sure Julie and Candy, have had numerous reasons to realize the truth and the reality of the words of Psalm 121."

"Now, these God-sent, God-graced, God-gifted reflections of everyday life are yours to share as well through the pages of this exceptional devotional as we each "lift up our eyes to the hills" here in the midst of God's Cathedral, again and again and again. As one member of our congregation says so often and so well, "this is a very special place." Read this book and you will understand that truth."

> Rev. Rick Underwood, Lake City, Colorado
> Pastor, Community Presbyterian Church

"For any woman who needs to be uplifted and to see things through a positive light, this is the book for you! These girls know how to see God working through nature and draw a clear picture of the mountains and make you feel as though you were right there sitting by a quiet brook, communing with God."

> Bobbie Clark and her husband Steve have been missionaries for 38 years, 20 years in Honduras, and now 18 in Cuenca, Ecuador

"I don't read devotions or most religious things, but **Mountain Devotional** is an exception. Perhaps it is because the writers often use nature as a takeoff, or it could be because of the sparkling writing! Whatever the cause it is an exception! I felt uplifted after reading it. Happy reading!"
    Mary Stigall, Lake City Colorado resident, former teacher, author and director. Mary started the Cabin Fever Players and the Arts Council — now Lake City Arts

"Living in the small, remote town of Lake City high in the Rockies provides many experiences that most of us former city dwellers have never before encountered. In each wonderful situation and phenomenon, Julie and Candy have reminded us of our need to rely on God and discover his amazing love for us."
    Faye Askew, Lake City, Colorado resident, former school teacher, business owner and active church volunteer

"For those of us who are blessed to live here in the Rocky Mountains, this devotional appropriately reminds us that while we are rewarded with a constant panorama of God's grandeur and majesty, our true joy comes from serving the Lord with thankfulness, faith and grace in good times and bad. This book celebrates both the internal and external love that God has for his children, bigger and better than any mountain we can imagine!"
    Sue Uerling. Executive Director, Six Points Evaluation and Training, Gunnison, Colorado

"Julie and Candy take us on a wonderful mountain trip that reaches those thin places where one can experience the immense love and compassion God has for us all. We need not fear old age, illness, the chances and changes of life, for our eternal God eternally embraces us with compassion and love."
"While attending the University of Colorado at Boulder I saw my first mountains, the Rockies. What a wonderful reminder of how to expand our knowledge of God's love walking those mountain trails. Now, wherever we live, all readers can walk in the mountains, as this is a devotional to turn to again and again."
>   The Rev. Sharla J Marks, Deacon, Saint Albans Episcopal Church, ECUSA Diocese of Fort Worth, Texas, Sharla is a chaplain at UT Arlington, and a member of the dioceses Executive Council. Soon to be a first time grandmother to twins!

"So much of life comes in moments, little slices, and short impressions. Julie and Candy have the ability to take these moments and polish them so that they shine and become praises. The writers know and feel that the mountains are special because everywhere you look there is the touch of God. This is not an ordinary devotional, it is a book that shows the reader how to praise God, one in which your thoughts bounce back and forth between scripture and those little slices of life in the Rocky Mountains. **Mountain Devotional** is a delightful set of reflections."
>   John W. Roose, PhD, Lake City, Colorado resident, retired philosophy professor at Trinity Christian College, Palos Heights, Illinois

Mountain Devotional

...He went up apart to pray

By

Candy Beebe and Julie A R Stephens

Table of Contents

Introduction p6
Why write? p8
Everything Love p9
George Darley p11
Six Points p13
Waterdog p17
Thompson Lake p20
First Love p22
Mother's Day p24
True earthly love p26
Worship God p27
God's Word p29
Why Worship God p31
God's Love p33
Natalie's funeral p34
Joy p35
Joyful journal p36
Joy in work p37
Christmas Songs p39
Joy in living p41
Bluebirds p42
Off Season Joy p44
Grandchildren p46
They are watching p47
Wee Care p49
Joy in nature p51

Birthdays p53
Peace p54
Recharge p56
God's Peace p57
Fall Colors p58
Simplicity p60
Sow and Reap p61
Hope, Joy, Peace p63
Eagles p65
Ordinary Time p67
Dandelions p69
The Comforter p71
Tents p73
Rain p75
Hummingbirds p77
The Gift p79
Going to Court p81
Vision p83
Health Fair p85
Alpine Gulch p86
Patience p88
Growing Old p90
Retirement p92
Balloon Festival p94
Fourth of July p96
Makeover – Part 1 p98
Makeover – Part 2 p100

Slowing down p125
Simple pleasures p101
Leanin' Trees p102
Kindness p104
Golden Rule p106
Bear Country p108
Bear Friends p110
Annuals p112
Workspace – Part 1 p114
Workspace – Part 2 p116
Goodness p118
Independence p120
Perfect Goodness p122
Goodness in rest p124
Volunteering p126
Staying light longer 138
Whitmore Falls p128
River Access p130
Pentecost Sunday p132
Walk in Clouds p134
Rainbows p136
Unpretentiousness p139
Faithfulness p140
God is Faithful p150
Stinger Band p142
NOT a Trail p144
A Foreign Land p146
Polaris p148
Pretty Feet p151
Charms p152
Thanksgiving p154

Acts 1:8 church p156
Memorial Day p158
Leave No Trace p160
Faithful p162
Gentleness p164
Gentle Pleasures p165
Cairns p166
Powderhorn Lakes p168
Sleepless – Part 1 p170
Sleepless – Part 2 p171
God's Courts p172
Wilderness Wisdom p174
Providence p176
Church p178
Self Control p180
Teach us to number our days p182
Self esteem p183
Peak Experience p184
Using Time Wisely p194
On Playing God p186
My Dog Kate p188
Little Surprises p190
Garage Sale p192
Hidden Dangers p196
Iron People p198
Hope p200
Pray Always p201
The Difference p202
About the Authors p203
Scripture Index p204

Introduction

The San Juan Mountains of southwestern Colorado are among the least known and least visited of the Colorado Rockies, yet they are thought by many, especially those who live here, to be the most beautiful and serene. It is against this backdrop that Candy Beebe and Julie Stephens present **Mountain Devotional.**

In a time that American Christianity seems focused on large churches seating thousands, the authors take us along on quiet adventures far from crowds and traffic and even roads. Centered in the USGA designated most remote country in the lower 48 they lead us toward a sense of prayer and peace that Jesus must have felt when he climbed, often alone, toward a special experience of the Holy.

While Jesus was hardly a 'mountain man' in the modern sense, his attraction to them almost reminds one of John Muir's well known quotes, "The mountains are calling and I must go." What called Jesus to these special places? And may it, if we listen closely, call us as well?

Often, Jesus led his disciples to a mountain. At the conclusion of his earthly ministry they went on their own to a mountain "...to which Jesus had directed them." There they encountered him.

In this devotional, though they may at first seem to be simply about a bear or rocks or birds or sky, we too may encounter the Lord himself. That is the purpose, after all, of **Mountain Devotional.**

Ed Nettleton
Lake City, Colorado May 2013

The Rev. Dr. Edwin Nettleton was ordained an Episcopal priest in 1966. Ed and Mary have been married 53 years. They came to Lake City, Colorado in 1991, where Ed is the victor of St. James. He is recently retired as chief of the volunteer fire department. He is an active pilot and outdoorsman, a Benedictine Oblate and has written numerous published essays and articles. Ed's first book is titled: *Why Were You Searching For Me? And 133 Other Questions Jesus Asks Each of Us.*

For I know the plans I have for you," declares the LORD, "plans to prosper you and not to harm you, plans to give you hope and a future.
Jeremiah 29:11 (NIV)

Why write this book

From Candy:
Upon arriving in Lake City, my husband, our daughter Kelly and grandson Koty spent many hours hiking various trails, especially the trails on Round Top. As we would make our treks something would happen, like stepping on a loose rock, or grabbing a dead tree to keep from falling. Various incidents would make me think of lessons to be learned. God speaks to us in so many ways, if we open "the eyes and ears of our heart." These few devotions are some of the insights God has shown me. My prayer is that these thoughts will bless and challenge.

From Julie:
Candy and I are both very much alike and very different so this volume will be much better written by the two of us than if it was either of us alone.

This devotional was written by laypeople with the hope that it appeals to everyone who loves nature, the mountains, Lake City in particular, loves God and want to think more about God somewhat gently each day and who ponder the eternal question: what is the purpose of life.

The book is organized by topics on the fruit of the Spirit. Even if the Holy Spirit is not a consideration for the reader the gifts are!

But the fruit of the Spirit is **love, joy, peace, patience, kindness, goodness, faithfulness, gentleness and self-control***. Against such things there is no law.* Galatians 5:22-23 (NIV)

Love

Everything comes back to love. There are two commandments: Love God and Love everyone else.

Everything comes back to love.

Oh my! So as I am thinking and writing and contemplating and meditating... I had an epiphany! And this is the crux of everything.

While I expect more from my marriage than I do any other relationship it finally occurred to me that my husband has that same right.

I have been too concerned about having been hurt rather than being concerned about me having caused hurt. I have been too concerned about me being loved rather than about me loving.

Hatred stirreth up strifes: but love covereth all sins. Proverbs 10:12

God, keep me growing on this amazing journey! Help me just concentrate on your command to show love. Help me be more loving and let you handle the rest. I already feel more peaceful.

As in the prayer of St. Francis...Lord, grant that we may not so much seek to be loved as to love...

Love is patient, love is kind. It does not envy, it does not boast, it is not proud. It is not rude, it is not self seeking, it is not easily angered, it keeps no record of wrongs. Love does not delight in evil but rejoices with the truth. It always protects, always trusts, always hopes, always perseveres. Love never fails.
1 Corinthians 13:4-8 (NIV)

We humans will fail again and again and again BUT if we are living truly authentic lives as a growing work in progress we will want to turn away from our selfishness as we grow to care more about others than ourselves, which is love. We must consistently show love in our actions, for words without consistent, loving actions are meaningless.

A herd of elk in winter

George Darley

For he chose us in him before the creation of the world to be holy and blameless in his sight.
Ephesians 1:4 (NIV)

George and Alexander Darley, missionary pastors to the San Juan's, arrived in Lake City in 1876 with the intention of building the first church on Colorado's Western Slope. They petitioned the presbytery for the organization of a Presbyterian church in Lake City. After electing elders and deacons it was decided to build a church as soon as possible.

Work on the 20x40 frame building in August of 1876; it was dedicated on November 18, 1876. The church was built before the town's courthouse or school building. Darley led the young church; however, it was not his only pulpit. He walked across the San Juan's to preach in mining camps and could frequently be found proclaiming the gospel in saloons of the mining boom days.

George Darley is a great example of how God chooses to work through people to accomplish His eternal purposes in the world. God calls individuals into a relationship with Himself so that He can use them to accomplish His purposes.

When God was about to destroy every living thing on earth, He called Noah to preserve life and repopulate the earth. When God was ready to deliver His people from Egyptian bondage, He called Moses to lead. The New Testament is filled with examples of God choosing people to accomplish His purposes.

We see men and women in Scripture as "superheroes" with great abilities. However, when God called them, they were ordinary men, women, children, carpenters, farmers, shepherds, servants, fishermen, tax collectors, prostitutes, and foreigners who simply had an obedient heart.

God does not need humans to accomplish His work; however He desires and is determined to involve His people. He calls individuals like Darley, like you and me. Then He empowers us to be instruments through which He continues to accomplish His eternal purposes.

Can you see any area in which God is calling you? How are you going to respond?

The distinctive shape of Uncompahgre Peak

Six Points

The following article about Six Points was first printed in the Lake City **Silver World** "Life From My View" by Julie Stephens, June 14, 2013. Copies of this devotional have been donated by the authors to Six Points thrift store in order to bring more awareness to their ongoing mission that helps mentally challenged adults live full lives through working in the store.

Life From My View

Who doesn't love getting a bargain? Being a fervent reader who gives children's books away, I happily spend the whole dime for beautiful, children's books, sometimes looking brand new!

Since I'm all about 'being green', and I get enjoyment from a pretty presentation, I find baskets are lovely gifts in themselves, an alternative to gift bags and 'green', as little to no wrapping paper is required.

Baskets also make a pretty, kitchen counter display for fruits and veggies, an easy to find home for lotions, bath oils, and soaps in the powder room, and baskets hold small toys for young visitors. I usually find pretty baskets from between a quarter to a dollar.

Yesterday, I bought a nice-looking, comfortable, wooden $4 chair with an upholstered seat. My husband agreed that it was a great match for the desk it now accompanies.

This was six or seven years ago, but my all time best deal: two washable silk pant suits. One suit had a Neiman Marcus label, and the other from Saks Fifth Avenue. They were $1 each, and it was a half-price day, so it was like paying a quarter for each piece of clothing from these legendary stores!

My style is a combination of classic and eclectic. I wear what is comfortable and what pleases me without giving a thought to fashion, and yet, continually, I am complimented on my finds!

While I can see my 'deals' getting harder to come by with giving away this treasure, I do like to be helpful, so letting those of you who do not know about this 'prize' in on the mystery, is a win-win!

Likely it is not possible to live in Lake City (or of course, Gunnison) even part-time without being blessed by *6 Points Thrift Store*. Certainly, if you are a shrewd shopper, and even more so if you want to be blessed.

How often and easily do we complain, and yet, how much harder could our lives be but by grace?

The mission of *6 Points* is to provide education, training, assistance, and support to all adults with special needs and their families in Gunnison and Hinsdale Counties, such that these individuals reach their highest functioning levels and become integrated into our society as independent, productive, contributing citizens. Further, their mission is to advocate for these individuals and increase the awareness of all residents concerning the special needs of the disabled in our community.

Besides the exceptionally low prices, every weekday has even more savings: Monday, bicycles are half price, Tuesday, appliances are $2 off with a minimum $5 purchase, Wednesday is 25% off all electronics, Thursday all books are half price (that's half off the dime for soft back, children's books and the quarter for hard back, children's books, as well as half off the dollar for hard back, adult books and the fifty cents for paper backs), and Friday is 25% off the furniture (Though I went ahead and bought my terrific, little, $4 chair on a Wednesday.) To top off all of these savings, folks 55 and older always get a 10% discount and periodically *6 Points* has a store wide, half-price sale for a specific time frame, usually lasting about a couple of weeks.

For those of you buying a vacation home, this is the first place to look for setting up housekeeping. For those of you selling a vacation home *6 Points* is also a great place to donate! Think of donating when spring cleaning out your closet or updating your wardrobe or deciding you really never are going to use the pasta machine you got for a gift.

While they take furniture that could use some tender loving care, please be diligent with donations and only bring clothing in the condition that you would wear it out and about. *6 Points* clients joke with shoppers, invite us to bible studies, look forward to vacation, thrive with employment, and will flourish all the more in the grand, new building.

While the current address and phone number is 320 S 14th St., Gunnison, CO 81230, (970) 641-3081, on April 18th *6 Points* hosted a groundbreaking ceremony for its new facility. Fundraising efforts are underway to raise about $800,000 to fully fund the construction. *6 Points* continues to seek donations of cash and to submit grant applications until the final goal is met. Certainly, the community will get involved in some of the planned fundraisers this summer.

The new store will to be located directly west of the Gunnison Recreation Center. This means we can work out and shop for smaller sizes all in one fell swoop!

Waterdog
God's Word is a life style

This is the covenant I will make with the house of Israel after that time, declares the Lord. I will put my laws in their minds and write them on their hearts. I will be their God, and they will be my people.
Hebrews 8:10 (NIV)

Waterdog Lake Trail begins on the edge of Lake City. The initial part of the climb was intense rocky hillside and through an Aspen grove that becomes less taxing as the trail ends at scenic Waterdog Lake. This is a good spot for fishing, camping or a picnic. It is also a beautiful area during the change of fall colors in mid-September.

There are great views of Lake City from the trail. However, what impressed me about this trail were the initials carved in many of the trees that lined the path. DC and J Hunt. Making inquiry it was easy learned who had committed the deed. (Note: Making one's presence known through the carving of initials at one time was a common practice and of offense to no one. This is not true now.) I asked DC about it and he laughed and told me each time he and J Hunt walked that way they would leave their mark. I knew these two were friends and have traversed many of the trails of Hinsdale and Mineral Counties.

God first told his people the importance of His word.

Fix these words of mine in your hearts and minds; tie them as symbols on your hands and bind them on your foreheads. Teach them to your children, talking about them when you sit at home and when you walk along the road, when you lie down and when you get up. Write them on the door frames of your houses and on your gates, so that your days and the days of your children may be many in the land that the LORD swore to give your forefathers, as many as the days that the heavens are above the earth. Deuteronomy 11:18-21(NIV)

See the verbs—tie them, wear them, teach them, talk about them, write them and remember them. But this was not enough.

This is the covenant I will make with the house of Israel after that time, declares the LORD. I will put my law in their minds and write it on their hearts. I will be their God, and they will be my people.
Jeremiah 31:33 (NIV)

God knows that always having His Word before us was not enough. It had to be put in our minds and written on our hearts. God's Word is a life style. It is how we think, what we eat, and what we breathe. It is what and who we are becoming, conformed to the image of Christ.

"Most merciful God, we confess that we have sinned against you in thought, word, and deed, by what we have done, and by what we have left undone. We have not loved you with our whole heart; we have not loved our neighbors as ourselves. We are truly sorry and we humbly repent. For the sake of your Son Jesus Christ, have mercy on us and forgive us; that we may delight in your will, and walk in your ways, to the glory of your Name. Amen." (BCP)

It is important in living a full life to keep moving forward, to keep being a good work in progress and to do that we must be aware of our sins — not our trespasses or our transgressions but our SINS and yet balance that knowledge with God's mercy and forgiveness.

It is OK to go, on occasion, out in the garden and eat worms. It is not OK to stay there. Pray. Meditate. Listen. Make changes. Move forward.

"Almighty God have mercy on us, forgive us all our sins through our Lord Jesus Christ, strengthen us in all goodness, and by the power of the Holy Spirit keep us in eternal life. Amen." (BCP)

Waterdog Lake

Thompson Lake Trail — The Way

Jesus answered, "I am the way and the truth and the life. No one comes to the Father except through me. John 14:6 (NIV)

Thompson Lake Trail, Crystal Trail and Larson Lake Trail each have their trailhead at I00F Cemetery, northwest of Lake City. Following a steep, jeep trail leads to the Forest Service boundary where the trail splits, and heading right leads to Thompson and Larson Lakes. Being a moderate, easily accessible and a half day excursion, this is a popular hike for visitors and residents alike.

It was in the fall the first time I hiked to Thompson Lake. The Aspen were shedding their leaves, leaving a golden carpet to lead the way. I thought of Dorothy and the yellow brick road that led to Oz and then home to Kansas. But too I thought about "The Way." In John 14 Jesus was encouraging the disciples, "Do not let your hearts be troubled, believe in God, believe also in Me." (vs.1) He tells them that they know the way that He (Jesus) is going. Thomas questions, "Lord, we do not where You are going, how do we know the way?" (vs.5) Jesus replies, "I am the way, and the truth, and the life, no one comes to the Father but through Me." (vs. 6)

THE WAY — Jesus uses "the" a definite article to distinguish Himself as "the only way." A way is a path, a trail, a route, a highway to God the Father. It is exclusive; no one can find God the Father except through Jesus. Peter reiterated this same truth to the crowd in Jerusalem, saying of Jesus, *Salvation is found in no one else, for there is no other name under heaven given to men by which we must be saved.* Acts 4:12 (NIV)

Our society rejects Christianity's claim to exclusivity declaring that there are many paths to the same place. Rejecting the truth does not nullify the truth. How do I know this statement is true? I know He is the Way from experience. I know it from my personal relationship with Him. I know it by His Spirit that lives inside of me. I know it through answered and unanswered prayer. I know it through joy and peace, sadness and sorrow, betrayal and forgiveness. His spirit bears witness with my spirit that I am a child of God.

Jesus said, "Follow Me." He is the path for your life. Trust in Him as Savior, NOW is the time.

Then shall they also answer him, saying, Lord, when saw we thee an hungered, or athirst, or a stranger, or naked, or sick, or in prison, and did not minister unto thee? Then shall he answer them, saying, Verily say unto you, Inasmuch as ye did it not to one of the least of these, ye did it not to me. And these shall go away into everlasting punishment: but the righteous into life eternal. Matthew 25:44-46

The Lord's Work is as straightforward and as multifaceted as is helping, being of service to others and God tells us that faith and works go hand in hand together. Words alone are meaningless. Lake City offers as many different opportunities to volunteer and help, as there are diverse people with various talents. Look. Ask. Work.

First Love

When I declared my love for him at our wedding, I was clueless to the meaning of, "I will love you till death parts us." When I brought each of my babies home from the hospital I "thought" I loved them but until it was tested in the rebellious teen years, then I KNEW I loved them. That's MATURE LOVE not the silliness of "first love."

I think of mature love as that which is tested and proven over time; love that remains and actually thrives in sickness and in health, richer or poorer, in happiness or sorrow. Flaws in character are accepted. Wrongs are endured and forgiven. A depth of feeling that chooses to love in spite of all we know about the other.

1 John 4:19 tells us that Jesus "first" loved us. Now I need to rethink my position on first love. Add to this the charge Jesus made against the church at Ephesus, "Yet, I hold this against you: You have left your first love." If Jesus feels strongly about "first love" this is a serious grievance against the church. What is it about first love that is so important that we keep it?

First love is passionate by nature and dominates all other issues in one's life. When a man and woman fall in love they want to spend every waking moment together, get to know everything there is to know about the other. They want to bring pleasure to each other; laugh together, comfort each other and share emotions, activities, and time. There is passion and thoughts about the other that dominate everything else.

This is what the Church at Ephesus had lost, its passion. There "love" for Jesus had become routine, "Ho-hum", just an everyday thing accepting the relationship as something taken for granted.

Jesus is saddened; it breaks His heart when we leave our first love. This first love for Jesus is not something we lose, but something we leave.

Love is a choice. Each day choose to let our thoughts be dominated by His thoughts or think about what we want to think about. We choose to read God's Word or not, to share our testimony or not, to pray or not, to lie or not, to obey His commands or not — and the list goes on and on. Each choice brings us closer to whom or what we love most.

Examine your heart. Have you left your first love? What can you do about it?

Mother's Day

"A mother is not a person to lean on, but a person to make leaning unnecessary." Dorothy Canfield Fisher

As I write we have just celebrated Mother's Day. My husband and I live in Colorado. Our grown son lives in Ohio and our grown daughter lives in Texas. Since we love each other we stay connected by phone, email, Internet video and real, face to face visits. Because I LOVE our children I taught them to be thankful, thoughtful and independent.

Irresponsible is the parent who spoils his child. Spoiling does not show love. To raise a person so that they think *their* feelings, *their* desires and *their* thoughts are most important is heartbreaking, neglectful parenting.

Unnecessarily difficult will be life for spoiled people who do not grow out of being self-absorbed.

While I worked hard for my academic and professional accomplishments and am very proud of them, my most rewarding accomplishments are my long, loving marriage (from which my children have also benefited) and my thoughtful, thankful, independent, kindhearted, grown children.

Teaching our children that it was not a beautiful store bought card with their signature that I wanted but it was and is their heartfelt words that I longed to receive. Over the years, this has been a lovely benefit for their dad and for me. Here are some of the loving sentiments I received from my grown son and daughter this Mother's Day:

"Mom! I am excited for our upcoming adventures and proud of all of your great recent accomplishments!"

"Mom! I'm so glad you guys were able to come visit us. It was wonderful to have you here. I'm proud of you and dad for figuring out this new stage of life. God has blessed us richly."

Train up a child in the way he should go: and when he is old, he will not depart from it.
Proverbs 22:6 (KJV)

True earthly love

I have heard it said that a couple cannot begin to know what love truly is until they have been married a quarter of a century.

To my beloved husband:

Our Love is the mountain that feels blinding snow
storms sometimes cold but never shattered
Our Love is the everlasting guide of the stars Our
Love is the cherry sunset
and the peach sunrise
Our Love endures like the wildflowers
that only appear to have died
but always return.

As many couples do, my husband and I had the Biblical Love Verse of First Corinthians read at our wedding and as many couples we are still working on it decades later. The key is to keep working at it! We keep working to grow and improve because we are no longer children.

When I was a child, I talked like a child, I thought like a child, I reasoned like a child. When I became a man, I put childish ways behind me. Now we see but a poor reflection as in a mirror; then we shall see face to face. Now I know in part; then I shall know fully, even as I am fully known. And now these three remain: faith, hope and love. But the greatest of these is love. 1 Corinthians 13:11-13 (NIV)

Worshiping God with all the Senses

Yet a time is coming and has now come when the true worshipers will worship the Father in spirit and truth, for they are the kind of worshipers the Father seeks. God is spirit, and his worshipers must worship in spirit and in truth. John 4:23-24 (NIV)

We have protestant churches and a catholic church in Lake City. However, we do not have a Greek Orthodox Church. Most of us know little about this part of Eastern Orthodox Christianity. The Eastern Orthodox Church officially called the Orthodox Catholic Church and commonly referred to as the Orthodox Church. It is the second largest Christian church in the world.

At the Annual Greek Festival at Annunciation Greek Orthodox Cathedral in Houston I attended a presentation by their priest, Father Michael. It included a video about Greek Orthodox beliefs and history. Members from their church gave interviews about their "connection" with their church. This was followed with opportunity to ask questions.

I learned that a portion of their service is in Greek, and that Greek language classes are provided for their constituents. The icons in the sanctuary are not prayed to, but rather point them to the worship of Christ. The worship songs are chants.

A dozen or so members talked about their church and referred to it as family, brothers and sisters, best friends and relatives. That is what church is supposed to be, an extended FAMILY.

Father Michael stated, "When we worship God, we worship Him with all of the senses." Images popped into my mind — incense, communion, the elaborate icons, stained glass, and intricate implements used in worship, listening to the language the New Testament was written in; touch — a bond of fellowship. But then my mind jumped to that other sense we all have, our spirit, our soul that connects with God. The Father is looking for, seeking for those who will worship Him in spirit and in truth, your innermost self reaching out to Him and honoring Him for who He is.

Take an inventory of your worship. Are you worshiping Him with ALL of your senses? God is seeking for those who will worship Him in spirit and in truth.

God's Word Is Everlasting

Dictionaries and thesauruses are irresistible. I own at least 5 dictionaries and 3 thesauruses. One year for Christmas I requested a new dictionary. Christmas morning there it was in all its glory and weight — a Webster's *Universal Unabridged Dictionary.* I used it as I wrote letters, articles for newspapers and bulletins, essays, and documents for school and work.

Alas, now this dictionary is more than 20 years old and antiquated. Word meañings keep changing; new words are coined daily. Just listen to any politician or preacher.

Now with my trusty computer I persist in my quest to spell accurately. Spell check is a poor speller's mother of all inventions. With a click of a mouse I correct my spelling. But to add to my arsenal of tools for not making a fool of myself is dictionary.com. Wow! I can look up a word's meaning. With the snap, my computer will give me the correct pronunciation. With another click I can find the word's entomology. Need a synonym, antonym or even a rhyming word? It's just a click away.

John writes in 1:1 and 14, "In the beginning was the Word, and the Word was with God, and the Word was God. And the Word became flesh and dwelt among us, and we saw His glory, glory as of the only begotten from the Father full of grace and truth."

There are several truly cool things about this WORD. One, the meaning never changes. "Jesus Christ, the same yesterday, today, and forever." Unlike the words at dictionary.com, THE WORD never changes, never loses its power, never out of date or obsolete.

Secondly, we can always see this WORD when we look for Him. In using my dictionary I note the print has shrunk over the years and is hard to see. But when I am looking at THE WORD, the only thing that clouds my vision is my "own words", me.

Thirdly, THE WORD is better than dictionary.com. Getting to Him is not dependent on technology — no computer glitch — no WIFI needed. Sometimes I will type in a word and get the response "no result found." Not so with THE WORD. He is my friend that is with me always.

Lastly, THE WORD gives me insight by the power of the Holy Spirit. God the Creator is able to give me thoughts, desires, ambitions, inspiration; not from a machine but from the Living God — THE WORD.

All Scripture is God-breathed and is useful for teaching, rebuking, correcting and training in righteousness, so that the man of God may be thoroughly equipped for every good work. 1 Timothy 3:16-17

Why Worship God

O come, let us worship and bow down; let us kneel before the LORD, our Maker! Psalms 95:6 (KJV)

When I was a teenager, I did not understand why God would want to be worshiped. When I was a child I understood as a child. Corinthians 13:11 As a parent I understand wanting some recognition and thanks, recognition of the sacrifices their dad and I made and a grateful heart for those sacrifices.

Having raised children has helped me in my understanding of God. I now completely comprehend worshiping the Lord Almighty, Creator of All, as we try to give thanks for our lives, our blessings and salvation.

Thou art worthy, O Lord, to receive glory and honor and power: for thou hast created all things, and for thy pleasure they are and were created.
Revelation 4:11 (KJV)

Having an authentic relationship with my grown kids is awesome! I will always and forever be their mom but they are no longer children, our relationship is more of a real connection as we are all adults. I think that's how it is with God now because when we really worship God we are outside of ourselves rather than, like children listing off our wish list as if we are talking to Santa. Just as my grown children feel closer to their dad and me with somewhat of an understanding of the sacrifices we made for them, we draw closer to God when we thank and praise Him.

Come near to God and he will come near to you.
James 4:8 (NIV)

Community Presbyterian Church — Lake City

God's Love

For my thoughts are not your thoughts, neither are your ways my ways, saith the LORD. For as the heavens are higher than the earth, so are my ways higher than your ways, and my thoughts than your thoughts. Isaiah 55:8-9 (KJV)

Part of a letter to a beloved friend:

Dear One,
I wish I could say that since I've been through what you are going though I know what helps...I wish I could say here my friend just do this...but I don't have the answer...the only thing that makes our lives work is work...feeling like we are not just doing busy work but we are doing what God wants of us and while OUR hope is that we are making a difference, WE may not be able to see or feel that but it is my experience that we do know when we are where God wants us, that much is clear.

The feeling that we are making a difference...that comes from us, being satisfied with where God wants us instead of thinking that there has to be more.

I have lots and lots of questions. I think that there are 200,000,000 questions and only 11 answers. However, I figure the creator of this amazing universe knows what He's doing.

For the LORD God is a sun and shield: the LORD will give grace and glory: no good thing will he withhold from them that walk uprightly. Psalm 84:11(KJV)

Natalie's funeral

Like a chapter out of a novel or a scene from a movie was Natalie's funeral, but this was real life. A brisk autumn afternoon in a grove of aspens shimmering gold in the sunlight, deer nearby and birds singing in the treetops, prayers spoken and unspoken. We sprinkled her ashes in the wooded area, never to forget this unique woman or this memorial service.

While too many able body folks ruin their health themselves and complain about their aches and pains, usually cheerful artist Natalie so affected the many lives she came into contact with, that the name of the Lake City June art show has been renamed the Natalie Reeve Memorial Local Artist Show. The stunning aspect is that Natalie's triumphs and temperament were accomplished from her wheelchair.

In our last conversation Natalie relayed how the doctors had told her she must not come to the exceptionally high altitude of Lake City. Natalie confessed she, 'cried like a baby' and then pulling herself together said she would go anyway that coming here was like her heaven on earth and if she couldn't come any more then she was ready to die.

It was only natural that Natalie's memorial service, like her life, was set apart from the norm as the sunlight and autumn breeze came together to create a tender lullaby of aspen leaves, a flickering golden pathway and God's wild animals close by as in a fairy tale, saying good-bye to their sleeping princess.

Will you be missed? Remembered? Do you make a difference?

Joy

Praising Rocks

Blessed be the King that cometh in the name of the Lord: peace in heaven, and glory in the highest. And some of the Pharisees from among the multitude said unto him, Master, rebuke thy disciples. And he answered and said unto them, I tell you that, if these should hold their peace, the stones would immediately cry out. Luke 19:38-40 (KJV)

I live in the Rocky Mountains. If you have ever been here you are aware of how they came to be called the Rockies. There are rocks everywhere. The mountains seem to be carved of stone; there are boulders from peaks to pastures; rocks of every conceivable size, shape, and mineral.

While I was walking the other day and observing the terrain this scripture came to mind. Immediately, I could envision a thunderous praise as the small pebbles in "squeaky" tones lifting their voices in adoration, the larger stones shouting exultation and glory to the King, the boulders booming, "Holy, Holy, Holy!" For a moment I joined them in honoring the Creator, the God of All, the Lord or Lords.

Derek Prince wrote, "If you spend an hour in prayer, 50 minutes should be worship and praise and thanksgiving. Only 10 minutes should be spent in request."

If we keep quiet, the stones who know nothing of His love and grace might burst into cheers. Certainly we who know His great salvation can declare His praise. Take time now to praise God.

Joyful journal entry

Springtime!!! The still cold mornings and nights of our still snowy Rocky Mountain springtime is warming us all with her signs that winter has passed!

While it is too soon to plant my perennials, I find their color and fragrance such a joy on the afternoon deck and inside the house at night.

Today I managed a rather well balanced, joyful day! It began before dawn, accomplishing much work, reading the Gospel and praying with my husband, and then praying to and from my early swim. It was a blessing to watch and photograph a mama fox with her babies! The rest of the day was a good balance of writing and preparing a class, with occasional breaks, to walk the dogs and read my latest, enjoyable library find.

My husband and I took pleasure in our simple tasty dinner on English Garden Stoneware from Six Points thrift store, watching a sunset of lavender and scarlet, while Beethoven played.

If I were so aware of my blessings each day would I enjoy them less...I think not.

Joy in Work

If I can stop one heart from breaking,
I shall not live in vain;
If I can ease one life the aching,
Or cool one pain,
Or help one fainting robin
Unto his nest again,
I shall not live in vain.

Emily Dickenson

Recently I met an able-bodied 20-year-old man whose goal in life is not to work; this makes me so sad. Lack of motivation and increasing unemployment are dangerously related. Individual's bodily needs of food, shelter and clothing must be met. It is in order to obtain these that most people work. Just as important as food and shelter is the need of our soul to flourish with making a difference in life.

At the time of this writing England's Prince William and his wife Katherine are expecting the birth of their first child in a short time. Because of this news, William's mother Princess Diana comes to my mind.

Princess Diana and I were about the same age and had our children at the same time. She was always in the media.

What I found most admirable about this beautiful, famous, wealthy woman was that ultimately Princess Diana learned that showing compassion and working to make a difference was more fulfilling than gowns and crowns. As a truly loving, caring mother she made certain to show her children that there was life outside the palace walls.

At the end of her life she was on target to rid the world of landmines, showing her sons that royal celebrity could be a force for change.

Her message was well received as her son William decided to take on as the first project he ever assigned himself, a short term shelter helping homeless families and single adults develop individual plans that promote becoming self sufficient.

There are always opportunities to work. In Lake City, paid and volunteer work positions are offered on line, in the Silver World and sometime in shop windows. Even if someone does not need to work for food and shelter, there is great joy to be found in a job well done. Making a difference in the lives around us is nourishment for the soul.

The sluggard craves and gets nothing, but the desires of the diligent are fully satisfied.
Proverbs 13:4 (NIV)

Christmas Songs

And Mary said: My soul exalts the Lord, and my spirit has rejoiced in God my Savior. Luke 1:46-47

The Christmas Concert by the Lake City Community Choir is a gift to the citizens of Hinsdale County. After weeks of practice this talented group delights the hearers with the carols, timely classics, and hymns. Another musical Christmas treat is presented by the school children at the lighting of the town park tree and a lively, fun musical/play production. The steeple bells of First Baptist Church ring out carols each afternoon the weeks before Christmas. Christmas and music go together and rightly so for there are four songs in the book of Luke that are part of the nativity account.

Mary's Song: Gabriel announced to Mary God's plan for her life and of her aged Cousin Elizabeth's pregnancy. When Mary came to her cousins home, the babe in Elizabeth's womb leapt and she was filled with the Holy Spirit (Luke 1:41); Elizabeth was inspired to understand a supernatural significance to this reaction, even before Mary gave her the news, she knew Mary would have a child. Mary's response is a hymn of praise.

Zechariah's Song: The miraculous birth of John the son of Elizabeth and Zechariah was cause for song; "Zechariah was filled with the Holy Spirit and prophesied" Luke 1:67. After nine months of enforced silence, he praises the faithfulness of God.

Like Mary, Zechariah mentions that salvation was predicted, that it was part of the blessings promised to Abraham (Gen. 22:18) , and that God was keeping those promises.

Angels' Song: In the times of Christ, shepherds in general were considered second-class and untrustworthy. Yet, God sent angels to shepherds to announce His son's birth; a host of angels who burst forth into song with "Glory to God is in the highest."

Simeon's Song: We know little of this ancient man; just that he came into the temple and when he saw Mary and Joseph with the child Jesus he took Him in his arms and blessed God in song.

This Christmas season reread these four songs. L e t your heart join with them singing as you encounter God's greatest gift to man, His son Jesus.

Joy in Living

Happily we bask in this warm, September sun; which briefly masks all difficulty.

The air is different today, though hardening mountain winds still taste crisp and clean. The air is full of scents too rich and ripe to hold — summer folk's good-bye kisses, wildflowers appearing suddenly like early spring in a last rush from the soft, cooling rains, new books, erasers, expectations, and reminiscent of a steadfast timepiece, the glorious aspen; not early at all — actually, very precise. Like freshly polished windows, the days are clean and streaked with a morning haze.

My garden has dwindled. I have pulled away from that passionate connection summer brought with her. All of September's gardens have cooled down with morning frost, and yet, there is still the afternoon warmth — the last of the outside blossoming for another season. Red geraniums begin to line windowpanes. A few remaining summer peaches melt in my mouth like bits of joy.

As we struggle, progress is made, and while perfection is never reached, the effort is satisfying.

Another 'V' moves overhead. Another leaf blushes red. Moving more quickly, I rhythmically toss and stack cords of wood; a good tired, a prayer of thanksgiving.

Bluebird of Happiness

When times are good, be happy; but when times are bad, consider: God has made the one as well as the other. Ecclesiastes 7:14

The area around Lake City flourishes with Bluebirds. This is largely due to the efforts of Helmut Quiram. The "Lake Fork Bluebird Trail" was initiated in 1987 when 180 bluebird boxes were installed beginning at Lake City and extending north to the middle of Miller Flats. As the years progressed more and more boxes were added extending past Powderhorn, Blue Mesa Road, and Creede and many side roads in between. For years Mr. Quiram has checked the boxes for occupancy. His philosophy is "....Bluebirds have been around for thousands of years. They can take care of themselves if they can nest but they must have cavities in which to raise their young."

Cultures around the globe associate bluebirds with happiness. The bluebird is a commonly accepted symbol of cheerfulness, happiness, prosperity, health and home, good health, renewal, and spring. *Somewhere over the Rainbow* refers to the "bluebird of happiness." Disney captured this thought in *Zippidy Do Da.*

Happiness. Happiness is characterized by or indicative of pleasure, contentment, and joy. The word "happy" originated from *hap* "chance, fortune". The word haphazard has the same root as happy and means lack of order or planning; determined by chance. The connection seems to be that happiness is hit and miss, dependent on circumstances, and reliant upon chance.

Ecclesiastes 7:1 correlates "good times" with happiness. But the writer goes farther with his thought, whether times are good or bad, circumstances excellent or poor, we abound or in want, God made the one as well as the other.

Paul knew about both coming from God, and wrote: *I know what it is to be in need, and I know what it is to have plenty. I have learned the secret of being content in any and every situation, whether well fed or hungry, whether living in plenty or in want. I can do everything through him who gives me strength.* Philippians 4:12-13 (NIV)

Whatever comes your way today, tomorrow, whenever — both good and bad, God has allowed. The question is "What are we going to do with our circumstances?"

Be devoted to one another in brotherly love. Honor one another above yourselves. Romans 12:10 (NIV)

Joy in the 'off season'

Rejoice in the Lord always. I will say it again: Rejoice! Philippians 4:4 (NIV)

It was 7° on our north deck before the sun came rolling into our valley this morning, 6° yesterday, 2° Friday and 9° Thursday, I see a pattern here!

The cold does not deter my joy in living up here! I raise the morning shade and smile and think I LOVE it!!! I LOVE living up here!!! I live up here! I love that this quiet season is settling upon us. Talking to the dentist yesterday and I said that Hawaii is one of those places that is good to visit but I wouldn't want to live there. He knew just what I meant as his daughter and son-in-law lived in Maui for two years and they said the same thing in that after awhile a beach, though beautiful, is just another beach, unchanged. The change of seasons is valuable.

Today the sky is BLUE! It is cobalt! Sapphire! Morning glory blue! The sun is shining ~ *so* magnificently engaging!!! I live *here*, in God's cathedral.

The heavens declare the glory of God, and the sky above proclaims his handiwork. Psalm 19:1

You shall go out with joy
And be led out with peace;
The mountains and the hills
Shall break forth into singing before you,
And all the trees of the field shall clap their hands.
Isaiah 55:12

I hear my husband's song play on my phone...I smile. Appropriately I tell him I am writing about joy.

Then the LORD God said, It is not good for the man to be alone; I will make him a helper suitable for him. Genesis 2:18

The man who finds a wife finds a treasure, and he receives favor from the LORD. Proverbs 18:22

American Basin

Grandchildren

Children's children are a crown to the aged, and parents are the pride of their children. Proverbs 17:6 (NIV)

Our son calls to video chat with our little grandson and I am filled with joy.

When a baby is born so is a grandmother!

Grandbabies make getting older joyful!

"We are not living in a private world of our own. Everything we say and do and think has its refection in everything around us." John Galsworthy

They Are Watching

Be imitators of God, therefore, as dearly loved children and live a life of love, just as Christ loved us and gave himself up for us as a fragrant offering and sacrifice to God... Ephesians 5:1-2 (NIV)

Kaydin is our 18-month-old grandson. While his dad was recovering from surgery, we had the delightful privilege of bringing him with us to Lake City.

Kaydin and I would go for short walks. When you are less than three feet tall, your steps are tiny. We struggled on the rough terrain enjoying the fall weather, picking up rocks and throwing them and all the fun things that toddlers do.

Kate, my dog joined us for our adventures. Kate is a cow dog. She spends her time fetching — balls, toys, sticks, anything you can toss she will fetch. She never tires of this activity. On our walks Kaydin and I took turns amusing Kate with the tennis ball. Kaydin would throw the ball a few inches to a few feet and Kate excitedly retrieved the treasure.

However, I do not care to touch the slobbery ball and therefore I would kick it. After a few rounds I noted that Kaydin no longer wanted to pick up the ball, but attempted to kick it, just like me. Eighteen months old and he is imitating my actions.

Paul writes to the church at Ephesus, "Imitate God, therefore, in everything you do, because you are his dear children." The King James Version states it, "Be ye therefore followers". We are to follow God by being like Him, imitating God. The Greek word signifies to "impersonate" others — assuming their gait, mode of speech, accent, carriage, etc.; and it is from this Greek word that we have the word mimic. Our American concept of mimic is often used in a ludicrous sense, yet here it is to be understood in a very solemn sense. Our whole conduct is to be like that of our Lord. We are to imitate him in all of our actions, words, spirit, and inclinations; imitate him as children do their parents, and remember that you stand in the relation of beloved children to him.

The word "therefore" connects the thought of how we are to imitate the Father. Read chapter four of Ephesians and make a list of the ways you are to be like the Father. And yes you can do it—verse 23-24, "Instead, let the Spirit renew your thoughts and attitudes. Put on your new nature, created to be like God — truly righteous and holy."

Wee Care

Lo, children are an heritage of the LORD... Psalm 127:3 (KJV)

Wee Care is the only state approved child care facility in Hinsdale County. Just as its name asserts it provides care for the counties youngest (wee) citizens and makes the statement that this community (we) cares about its children. County and town government along with Lake City Community School, numerous community organizations believe so strongly in the importance of children and families that they invested heavily in support of the construction of a new facility in 2012. These perceptive individuals understood the significance of providing the very best possible care, nurture, and early childhood education.

This Psalm tells us that children come directly from God as a gift and God takes personal responsibility for the creation of life in the womb (Genesis 30:17; 33:5; 48:9)

God uses children to teach us adults, patience, understanding, love, faithfulness and much more. They help develop the fruit of the spirit in our lives. Children hold us accountable when we fail in the values we seek for them to have.Children remind us that God has not given up on us humans.

God blesses adults who show the love of Jesus to children. Jesus declared in Matthew 18:5 that whoever welcomes a little child like this in my name welcomes me. Then he gives this warning...

But if anyone causes one of these little ones who believe in me to sin, it would be better for him to have a large millstone hung around his neck and to be drowned in the depths of the sea. Matthew 18:6

Jesus taught that the kingdom of God is like a little child (Mark 10:15) and that those who wish to enter the kingdom must do so as children (Matthew 18:1-5) that the child is symbol of Christ like humility, and that a father is not likely to give his child a stone when asked for bread, a snake when asked for fish, or a scorpion when asked for an egg. (Luke 11:11-13) These references depict a society that values children.

You can tell a lot about a community, a culture, a society by the way it treats their children. Jesus loves children, and those who harm children will answer to him.

"Almighty God, heavenly Father, you have blessed us with the joy and care of children: Give us calm strength and patient wisdom as we bring them up, that we may teach them to love whatever is just and true and good, following the example of our Savior Jesus Christ. Amen." (BCP)

Joy in Nature

Aspen Trees

The body is a unit, though it is made up of many parts; and though all its parts are many, they form one body. So it is with Christ. 1 Corinthians 12:12 (NIV)

Aunt Birdie had me painting Aspen trees years before I ever saw one. She had traveled around the world but as she would describe the golden leaves, fluttering in the breeze, her eyes would light up with wonder. She instilled in me a desire to see these "trembling quakes" for myself.

Lake City is filled with the fascinating Aspen. These striking trees are remarkable. Aspen grow in large, cloned colonies. An Aspen tree above ground appears to be one distinct individual tree, but underground it spreads by means of root suckers. New stems that are new trees grow around the parent tree. It appears that these trees are distinct from each other, but underground they are interconnected and are all clones of the same plant; genetically one, but separate ascending trees. An individual tree may live for 40-150 years above ground and die, yet the root system lives on. Aspen can withstand forest fires because the root system is below the heat of the fire. Because the species does not flourish in shade, fire indirectly benefits aspen trees for it allows new trees to grow due to the increased sunlight in the burned landscape.

The Church, the body of Christ is "one" organism, one whole body, but many parts. Like the Aspen we appear on the outside as many entities, but we are genetically the same. We have one heavenly Father. We have "the family" resemblance to His Son Jesus Christ. We are interconnected by a powerful root system, the Holy Spirit that binds us and makes us one in Christ and one with each other.

On the surface we may appear a conglomeration, a hodge-podge of men, women, boys and girls with little in common but church attendance. But that is not reality. Our common "root", Jesus Christ fastens us together. Attacks from the enemy, like the fire for the Aspen, seem devastating. But the powers of hell will not and CANNOT conquer the Church. The fire's purpose is not to destroy but to allow us to flourish with the increased light, The Light of the World.

Praise and thank God for the body of Christ where He has placed you. Ask Him to help you thrive and grow to increase in the Light.

Birthdays

Birthdays are for joyfully celebrating! In Lake City, at St. James, Ed or Konrad bless those celebrating birthdays or anniversaries. I like to send this prayer to friends on their birthday:

"Watch over your child (name), O Lord, as their days increase; bless and guide them wherever they may be. Strengthen them when they stand; comfort them when discouraged or sorrowful; raise them up if they fall; and in their heart may your peace which passes understanding abide all the days of their life; through Jesus Christ our Lord. *Amen.*" (BCP)

"You are never too old to set another goal or to dream a new dream."   C. S. Lewis

Peace

Last night at dinner my husband and I were listening to a wonderful rendition of Aretha Franklin's 'What a friend we have in Jesus' and the line that captured our attention was something like: what a peace we often forfeit, what a needless pain we bare, all because we don't take everything to God in prayer...

While I am a firm believer in doing everything I can to help a situation, I am learning that I must then trust God, the Creator of all to be in control. Yes, people have free will but what a peace we often forfeit, what a needless pain we bare because we don't take everything to God in prayer...and trust HIM.

Do not be anxious about anything, but in everything, by prayer and petition, with thanksgiving, present your requests to God. And the peace of God, which transcends all understanding, will guard your hearts and your minds in Christ Jesus. Philippians 4:6-7 (NIV)

One of the numerous blessings of living here in God's Cathedral is that we can find many a sweet spot up in the mountains, in the forest, caught up in the clear and amazing constellations or beside the mint crested river and catch our breath away from the rough edges of our lives.

Be still, and know that I am God. Psalm 46:10

We pray for the peace of God several times during the church service at St. James.

Peacefulness: calm, tranquil.

"Almighty God, in giving us dominion over things on earth, you made us fellow workers in your creation: Give us wisdom and reverence so to use the resources of nature, that no one may suffer from our abuse of them, and that generations yet to come may continue to praise you for your bounty; through Jesus Christ our Lord. Amen." (BCP)

Escape and Recharge

Very early in the morning, while it was still dark, Jesus got up, left the house and went off to a solitary place, where he prayed. Simon and his companions went to look for him, and when they found him, they exclaimed: "Everyone is looking for you!"
Mark 1:35-37 (NIV)

Life is demanding. Each of us has so many roles that we are called on to fill — mother, father, breadwinner, chauffeur, coach, counselor, employee, employer, teacher, friend, confidant and on and on. Many times I have told my husband I feel like STRETCH ARMSTRONG. Stretch Armstrong was a rubber toy that kids could pull and tug everything on his body and then would pop back to his normal shape when the pressure was off. Unfortunately, I never "popped back".

The stress of demands can take its toll, physically, emotionally, and spiritually. That is why we need to take time to simply escape with God, alone and recharge — like you are doing right now, reading this. He wants to be with you and help you to slow down for a few moments and seek Him. It will give the two of you the chance you need to hang out together.

The Peace of God

An acquaintance died today. He was 31. He died just as most US middle class people are beginning to live grown-up lives with their careers, perhaps their own families and buying their first house. He died from a lifelong struggle with an incurable disease. He could not believe a loving God would create him just to suffer and die young, so he did not believe in God.

I cannot believe a merciful God would commend this young man for all eternity after his hell on earth.

And have mercy on those who doubt; Jude 1:22

Engineer Pass — Elevation 12,800

Fall Colors

There is an appointed time for everything; and there is a time for every event under heaven.
Ecclesiastes 2:16

It's started, ever so subtle like it does each year. A few yellow leaves on a branch of an aspen, the "postage stamp" just right of Round Top, the cool nip in the air—the changing of the seasons. Lake City and the surrounding area will soon become a colossal work of art as God's "painting" is revealed in a riot of orange, red, and yellow. It will last only a few weeks, then the bare trees and evergreens will await the winter snows that will then lead to spring and on again to summer.

Times and seasons are the invention of God.

Theologians and philosophers have much to ruminate about God's relationship to time:time is circular; God exists in the eternal present; God lives outside of time; the eternal "I AM." When I read their ideas it makes my head spin.

I think times and seasons were given by God for our benefit and enjoyment. Morning and evening, seasons, days and years are mentioned at the start of Genesis. "Process of time," "appointed time," "set time," "at that time" — there are 620 occurrences of the word *time*. The word *season(s)* is found 68 times as "an appointed time." These terms are always used in relationship to men or God's dealings with man.

Ecclesiastes chapter three gives readers a glimpse of God's use of time in the lives of us humans. In verse 3:1, it states that "there is a time for every event under heaven." There are seasons in our lives.

As Solomon wonders about the sovereign design of God he concludes that all the events of life are divinely appointed. This is mind boggling! All the events of my existence and yours are divinely appointed. (Psalm 139:16)

God in His eternal wisdom and foreknowledge knows about the events of our lives. Nothing that happens to us takes God by surprise. Our problem is that we see "time," as what is happening *now*, what we are facing *now*, and the season we are going through *now*.

But "God has set eternity in their hearts." Ecclesiastes 3:11

There is *now* the necessity for us to view times and seasons, but with an eternal perspective.

Simplicity

There is peacefulness in simplicity.

"And he said to them, Take care, and be on your guard against all covetousness, for one's life does not consist in the abundance of his possessions."
Luke 12:15 (ESV)

"Simplicity is the ultimate sophistication."
Leonardo da Vinci

I know that more is not better when it comes to things. I abhor clutter and yet I sometimes struggle with it. I want my favorite things around me. Yet I know while I find a few of my favorite things comforting, too many are distressing rather than a joy.

Do not lay up for yourselves treasures on earth, where moth and rust destroy and where thieves break in and steal, but lay up for yourselves treasures in heaven, where neither moth nor rust destroys and where thieves do not break in and steal. For where your treasure is, there your heart will be also.
Matthew 6:19-21 (ESV)

Sowing and Reaping

A Harvest of Righteousness

Peacemakers who sow in peace raise a harvest of righteousness. James 3:18 (NIV)

The growing season at above 8000 feet is short. The weather is dry early in the summer and then the monsoons hit. Local plant "aficionados" have told me if I plant seeds, start them inside and not to set them outside until the middle of June. This year I had one strawberry plant that produced six strawberries — yea! What if I had planted more? I had two cherry tomato plants that the deer decimated twice. By the time I found a safe spot for them the weather turned cooler. No tomatoes. I sowed four sunflower seeds. I passed them on to a friend. She had three gigantic blooms and reaped delicious seeds.

In the third chapter of James, the writer addresses those who thought themselves to be wise, wise enough to teach others. In giving them a description of wisdom, he wants them to understand what true wisdom entails — trusting God and His word and living the righteous life that God desires. Humility is wisdom (3:14) that reveals itself in a life of goodness, purity and peace toward other people.

Wisdom is evidenced by good behavior and deeds. Wisdom is a practical matter demonstrated by the way one lives. Wisdom is not something merely possessed in one's head, but shown in one's conduct.

The wisdom that we are to seek is from above (3:17) James contrasts the wisdom which is not from above, but earthly, natural, demonic and is exposed by its bitter envy and arrogance that leads to lies and disorder.

True wisdom comes from God himself and is expressed by purity, peace, gentleness, reasonableness, mercy and good fruits. It is unwavering and without hypocrisy. He concludes with "the fruit of righteousness is sown in peace by those who make peace." This connects peacemaking and righteousness. James wants peace for the church because peace is the environment in which righteousness can flourish.

Human anger and arrogance do not bring about the righteous life that God desires. What can you do to sow peace that you might reap a harvest of righteousness?

Hope Joy Peace

It is good to have such a hopeful morning. I slept for the first time in numerous nights; a loved one's surgery went well. Though it is -19° the sunlight is streaming through the windows of our famous deep blue sky days with the promise of warmth.

May the God of hope fill you with all joy and peace as you trust in him, so that you may overflow with hope by the power of the Holy Spirit.
Romans 15:13 (NIV)

We ask an awful lot of these mountains. We ask them to make us peaceful and happy as we come hot and worn out from the business of life. Yet when we take the time to sit and be still, when we inhale deeply and gulp in the flow of crisp mountain air, the change of outlook begins, the mountains stroke us with pines, aspen, wildflowers, wildlife, this is the beginning of peaceful happiness.

Outside, being quite alone with the mountain, it feels that all is as it should be, because as long as the mountains exist, there will be comfort and hope.

Today the rain kisses and caresses the mountains and trees and also gives the air a powerful sweetness, sweetness we can taste.

Tolstoy once said, "A busy summer balanced with quiet secluded nine months of life in the mountains, doing good and being useful to each other; then work which one hopes may be of some use; then rest, nature, books, music, love for one's neighbor — such is my idea of happiness."

I enjoy asking the vacationing folks, "How are you doing?" Most will smile and respond in a positive way. "Wonderful," I say, "As that's the only way you are allowed to be up here, otherwise, what's the point!" They usually get my message and smile broader, sometimes even laugh.

A cheerful heart is good medicine.
Proverbs 17:22 (NIV)

It was a funny moment, the elks mooned the camera.

Eagles

Know ye not, that so many of us as were baptized into Jesus Christ were baptized into his death? Therefore we are buried with him by baptism into death: that like as Christ was raised up from the dead by the glory of the Father, even so we also should walk in newness of life. Romans 6:3-4 (KJV)

It is not uncommon to see an eagle soar along the Lake Fork of the Gunnison River or at the Blue Mesa Reservoir. When I spy the magnificent bird of prey, I thank God for delighting me with its magnificent beauty.

The American bald eagle graces the Great Seal of the United States, American currency, and numerous other American items as a symbol. John F. Kennedy said, "The fierce beauty and proud independence of this great bird aptly symbolizes the strength and freedom of America."

The purpose of a symbol is to communicate meaning, especially a material object representing something abstract. The value of symbols depends on how we use them. If the underlying truth is kept in focus, a symbol can be a powerful tool to aid our memories and develop our understanding.

As Christians we experience the powerful symbolism of baptism to remind us of the truth of God's Word and the reality of our salvation. Water baptism symbolizes the death, burial and resurrection of our Jesus Christ.

Baptism is our identification with Christ. Water baptism gives the believer the opportunity to openly declare to others of their born-again experience; an outward sign of an inward grace.

The baptismal waters represent death to self and proclaim to heaven, earth, and hell, that the old you is dead. Coming up out of the water signifies being raised to new life in Christ.

Water baptism is an act of obedience for the believer. It should be preceded by repentance, a turning from our sin and selfishness, placing our pride, our past and all of our possessions before the Lord, giving the control of our lives over to Him.

Water baptism is basic Christianity, for every believer. If you have never "buried" your old, sinful nature and dedicated yourself wholly 100% to the Lord, don't wait any longer. Now is the time to be baptized in water.

Ordinary Time

For me, ordinary time is anything but ordinary! The simple joys of life are always the best. There is sacredness to daily living. Learning to be content is life's great lesson. To appreciate having work, clean laundry scented with sunshine, a small house with pets, books, writing paper, firewood, a glass of wine, a loaf of bread, a view, a bed and someone to love is being blessed beyond measure.

Folks are usually taken aback at the simplicity of our mountain house. It was built as inexpensively as possible, over three decades ago as a seasonal retreat. The incredibility amazing views are the center of attention and my spouse and I are blessed to call it home.

But godliness with contentment is great gain. For we brought nothing into the world, and we can take nothing out of it. But if we have food and clothing, we will be content with that. 1 Timothy 6:6-8 (NIV)

Finally, brethren, whatsoever things are true, whatsoever things are honest, whatsoever things are just, whatsoever things are pure, whatsoever things are lovely, whatsoever things are of good report; if there be any virtue, and if there be any praise, think on these things. Philippians 4:8 (KJV)

Every day will I bless thee; and I will praise thy name for ever and ever. Psalm 145:2 (KJV)

Dandelions

Make every effort to live in peace with all men and to be holy; without holiness no one will see the Lord. See to it that no one misses the grace of God and that no bitter root grows up to cause trouble and defile many. Hebrews 12:14-15 (NIV)

They show up each spring. This perennial is everywhere in Lake City; the park, along the highway and town streets, vacant lots and even in well groomed lawns. Hidden all winter they quickly brighten all of outdoors with their yellow polka dots — dandelions.

Dandelions are a nuisance, hording water and nutrients from grass. The taproot is deep, twisted, and brittle and unless it is removed completely, it will regenerate. A surfeit of dandelions simply means that the grass and the soil need attention.

The writer of Hebrews warns believers to not let the "root of bitterness" spring up to cause trouble and corrupt others. This imagery comes from Deuteronomy 29:18 *"I am making this covenant with you so that no one among you...will turn away from the LORD our God to worship these gods of other nations, and so that no root among you bears bitter and poisonous fruit."*

Verse 19 identifies the root: "Those who hear the warnings of this curse should not congratulate themselves, thinking, 'I am safe, even though I am following the desires of my own stubborn heart.' This would lead to utter ruin!"

Moses and the writer of Hebrews caution, that those in covenant with Christ cannot continue or return to live according to the "desires of your own stubborn heart." Christians are to cultivate faith and holiness. We must not neglect our great salvation but be vigilant to fight the fight of faith every day lest we become hardened and fall away.

This root of bitterness is much like the dandelion. The taproot — our own stubbornness — is twisted and hard. It steals nutrients stunting your relationship with Christ. The fruit of bitterness spreads like this weed and harms not only the body of Christ but all who come in contact with its poison.

The solution — focus on the soil — "the dirt in your heart". We each need to examine ourselves and approach our Lord with a contrite heart, humility, and submission to Christ.

The Comforter Has Come

Nevertheless I tell you the truth; It is expedient for you that I go away; for if I go not away, the Comforter will not come unto you; but if I depart, I will send Him unto you. And when He is come, He will reprove the world of sin, and of righteousness, and of judgment.
John 16:7-8

September in Lake City, the nights are getting cooler and the morning air crisper. There is smoke rising from a chimney or two. In preparation for winter I placed the down comforter on our bed. The next morning my husband looked at the comforter and said, "The comforter has come."

"The Comforter Has Come" is a hymn written by Frank Bottome, an American Methodist pastor. It first appeared in the hymnal, *Precious Times of Refreshing and Revival*, in 1890. Jars of Clay, a contemporary Christian group recently has recorded this timeless classic.

The Holy Spirit comforts the believer. The third person of the trinity was sent by the father to "run at our side and pick us up." 1 John 2:1 refers to Christ as our advocate. The word "advocate" is the same word as "comforter" in John 16:7, 8. Jesus is our advocate, or comforter, or the one who runs at our side to pick us up. This was especially true during His earthly life, but when He returned to heaven He sent us another comforter. John 14:16, 17 and 26, "And I will ask the Father, and he will give you another Comforter who will never leave you. He is the Holy Spirit, who leads into all truth.

The world at large cannot receive him, because it isn't looking for him and doesn't recognize him. But you do because he lives with you now and later will be in you. But the Comforter, Which is the Holy Spirit, Whom the Father will send in My name, He shall teach you all things, and bring all things to your remembrance, whatsoever I have said unto you."

The Holy Spirit came to be a helper for Christians. Jesus was the One Who ran to our side, but once He returned to heaven, He sent the Holy Spirit to do for all of us what He did when He was here. Still, according to 1 John 2:1, Jesus is still our comforter, so the Holy Spirit is not exactly a substitute but an additional one to run to our side. We need that "double whammy" of care and assistance.

Listen via the internet or look in a hymnal and reflect on the truth—"*The Comforter Has Come*. "

Tents

Now we know that if the earthly tent we live in is destroyed, we have a building from God, an eternal house in heaven, not built by human hands.
2 Corinthians 5:1 (NIV)

Many people like to camp in tents. It never ceases to surprise me when I am hiking a remote trail and spot a lone campsite tent or even a group of outdoors enthusiasts enjoying the beauty of the San Juan Mountains. I have read that when done properly with all the right equipment and knowledge about camping, it can be fun.

The most wretched nights of my life have been spent in a tent. Despite being fully clothed and using what I considered an adequate sleeping bag, I shivered in the cold and ached from the hardness of the ground. "I like to camp out at the Holiday Inn."

A tent is a temporary place to dwell. It is not home with a warm bed, cozy fire, comfy chair, and indoor plumbing. It is cold in the winter, hot in the summer, leaky in the rain, and can be blown away with the wind. With time it sags, it tears, it frays, and it rots, and is no longer usable.

The Bible likens our physical body to a tent. Paul writes that our earthly tent, our body is a temporary dwelling place in which our spirit lives and contrasts it with the eternal resurrection body. *"For indeed while we are in this tent, we groan, being burdened."* (vs. 4) Just like tents wear out with use, so does our fleshly body. It loses it newness and its usefulness. We can take vitamins and supplements, eat right, exercise, use age defying creams or even surgery, yet this body will one day die and be of no use to us.

This passage in 2 Corinthians 5 encourages us that God has given the Holy Spirit as a pledge of His promise of the resurrection. Like earnest money given as a promise of a purchase, God has given us the third person of the Trinity to live inside of us. We live here on this earth by faith in what lies ahead and what we cannot see. We use this body, this tent, for a brief place for our soul to live. One day, in the near future, we will be absent from this body and at home with God. In the mean time, our desire, our ambition, should be to live pleasing to Him.

Read 2 Corinthians 5:1-9 in different versions of the Bible. Think on this passage focusing on being pleasing to Christ.

"Don't be yourself - be someone a little nicer." — Mignon McLaughlin, *The Second Neurotic's Notebook*, 1966

Rain

It is early spring and it's raining! This sweetness hasn't been heard in a long, long time. And the rain isn't taken for granted. Either we were living through the drought of Texas, or if we were getting moisture in the mountains, it was too cold to rain.

This morning, with the threat of rain, Karen and I were talking in the post office about how, while we were very grateful for the rain, the day was promising, but it would really, really be nice if it rained this evening. My husband was outside painting the bell at St. James and Karen had plans for the afternoon.

The rain indeed came down after sunset! It doesn't work this way! Either the threat turns into rain or the sun comes out, but to have it threaten all day and rain in the evening, as we wished...that never happens! We are truly grateful Lord! Thank you for the rain and for the timing.

Decades ago, Lake City had daily summer showers like my home town of New Orleans, without the humidity, but it seems that rain cycle has been broken.

And he prayed again, and the heaven gave rain, and the earth brought forth her fruit. James 5:18

Finding such pleasure and peacefulness in this moment...the swish of a spring shower this evening, writing in the firelight with the rain gently, musically, as our backdrop, my husband reading nearby, our dogs lying at our feet...who cares what the rich people are doing tonight!

My husband just pointed out the interesting phenomenon that while it is raining in our valley looking up just a bit on Gold Hill it is snowing!

For as the rain cometh down, and the snow from heaven, and returneth not thither, but watereth the earth, and maketh it bring forth and bud, that it may give seed to the sower, and bread to the eater.
Isaiah 55:10 (KJV)

Uncompahgre Peak — Elevation 14,321

Hummingbirds

Blessed are they which do hunger and thirst after righteousness: for they shall be filled. Matthew 5:6

Hummingbirds delight us here in Lake City. These tiny jewels of the avian kingdom are amazing to watch. Flitting up and down, forward, backward and sideways, stopping in midair. Their aerial displays often look like dive bombers.

These migratory birds choose to visit and stay in Lake City for one reason—food. Their relentless demand for food is the result of their high-energy life-style.In the quest for reliable food sources, hummingbirds are extremely mobile, seeking flowers in the lowlands in spring and the mountains in summer. Hummingbirds consume more than their own weight in nectar each day, so they must visit hundreds of flowers daily. Hummingbirds are continuously hours away from starving to death and are able to store just enough energy to survive overnight. At the end summer the tiny species goes into a feeding frenzy as it prepares for migration.

In the Sermon on the Mount, Jesus says that those who hunger and thirst for righteousness will be filled. He is not speaking of ordinary hunger and thirst for food and drink but desires and appetites. We crave (hunger and thirst) for fulfillment, happiness, purpose, and love; all intangible things.

Many seek them through work, careers, and altruistic deeds. Others search for satisfaction in drugs, sex, pornography and other lusts of the flesh. Still others look for gratification in things or in fame. However none of these things truly satisfy this emptiness inside. Only God can fill that empty spot, that craving inside of each person. God and God alone is the source of fulfillment, purpose, love, and joy.

When God created Adam, He made him in His own image. He breathed into him the breath of life, which is His spirit. In Ecclesiastes, Solomon wrote that God placed eternity in our hearts. I think of it like this: There is a vacuum inside of every human. The only thing that can fill that emptiness is God. It is a 'God Spot'. We attempt to fill it in all kinds of ways, but it won't work. Only God truly fits there. That is what Jesus knew and told us how to fill that vacuum, "hunger and thirst for God. "If we do, God will not reject us, He will fill us. Read the Sermon on the Mount, Matthew 5-7. Ask God to give you a hunger and thirst for righteousness. A hunger and thirst for the living Christ.

The Gift

When Jesus heard this, he said to him, "You still lack one thing. Sell everything you have and give to the poor, and you will have treasure in heaven. Then come, follow me." Luke 18:22 (NIV)

Usually, the first Saturday in December begins the shopping, called "Christmas in Lake City." There are crafts for kids in the armory, the fruit cake toss in the park, carols by the children before the lighting of the tree, and a Christmas performance by the Lake City Stinger Band and the Lake City Lakettes. On this special day, many shops are open, warm and inviting, with tasty treats. There is a brass ensemble that goes from store to store to play music. It is a magical time, the way I picture Christmas long ago, in a simpler time. An additional pleasure is the winter snow, hints of an upcoming white Christmas.

I shop local, but it is impossible to get every gift I am looking for. What do you give to the person who has everything? We all have a family member or friend who seemingly has everything. Just such a person came to Jesus in Luke 18:18-27. A man asks, *"What must I do to inherit eternal life?"* He is respectable and religious, rich and righteous. He knows the law of God and is obedient to it. He has done what we find so difficult, to combine wealth and worship.

So what is missing? The answer suggested by Jesus is "nothing." This high achiever had missed the joy of having nothing, the simple innocence of being powerless and possession-less. Jesus prescription for what ails him is to give away everything and try nothing. Jesus offers him the gift of eternal life. He cannot receive it. Sadly, the man with seemingly everything, walks away grieving, trapped by his wealth; there is no happy ending for him. But what we find impossible, Jesus tells us, God makes possible. I want to believe that God might later have made possible a change for this devout man, that he might even have become a fellow believer and shared his story. Perhaps the grieving and sadness were the first steps to repentance?

Don't be trapped by anything that keeps you from fully surrendering to the Lord. If you are, pray for strength to let it go.

St. Rose of Lima Catholic Church — Lake City

Going to Court

My dear children, I write this to you so that you will not sin. But if anybody does sin, we have one who speaks to the Father in our defense — Jesus Christ, the Righteous One. 1 John 2:1(NIV)

As our fledgling country developed and spread west, law and order were paramount. For this reason courthouses were one of the initial buildings built in new townships. Hinsdale County Courthouse is Colorado's oldest courthouse that continues to be utilized for its original purpose.A framed building, it is representative of the local interpretation of the Italianate style with clapboard exterior, bracketed cornice, corner boards, frieze board, transoms, and narrow windows with crown molding. A curved stairwell leads to the upstairs courtroom that retains many original furnishings.

In September 1877, suffragette Susan B. Anthony spoke to a capacity audience at the courthouse. In April 1883, the historic trial of cannibal Alfred Packard also took place within its walls and today the original sentencing documents are available for view at the courthouse.

1 John 2:1 is one of many verses in the Bible that uses a governmental analogy. An advocate is one who pleads the cause of another; a person in a court of law; one who uses his influence in behalf of another by his request. The role of an advocate is to defend the accused and to secure justice and prevent conviction or argue for a pardon when a criminal has been justly condemned.

This is what Christ does for us. Mankind is rightfully condemned, "*For all have sinned...*" (Romans 3:23).

Guilt is already ascertained, the verdict is guilty, and death is certain. But Jesus defends us at the throne of grace, not for the purpose of preventing conviction, for He was condemned for us. He died in our place. Now as our advocate, He pleads His sin offering, as a condition, upon which we may be forgiven. His request is directed to a merciful God who accepts Christ as our surety, one who makes Himself responsible for us.

Christ longs to represent you before the Father. If you have not asked Christ to represent you before the Father, ask Him now.

Vision

Do you have eyes but fail to see, and ears but fail to hear? And don't you remember? Mark 8:18 (NIV)

My mother-in-law came to visit us here, once. Dammaw had never traveled far from her Louisiana roots, but after much urging and cajoling, we persuaded her to visit Lake City.

She had never seen a mountain up close and personal. She had never viewed a clear mountain stream or a raging waterfall like North Clear Creek Falls. Though the Aspen were bare of their foliage, she would stare back at their knotty black eyes. She would enjoy the simple pleasure of the boardwalks, rocky dirt streets, and quaint historic storefronts, or just sitting in the town park. For two months she never tired of seeing the sights, drinking in the vision, aware of God's hand in creation and in her life.

Another visitor came. We entertained him with the sights that had so delighted Dammaw. He commented, "It's the same ole, same ole." He had no vision to see and appreciate and bask in the wonders of His Maker.

There is a contrast among church attendees. One soaks in the presence of God with earnest worship, and giving with open hearts in obedience and love. They respond to the preaching of God's Word and power of the Holy Spirit. They joyfully share their lives encouraging others in word and deed, sharing their faith. They are involved and excited about Jesus and how He is working in and through the church, in their families, in their friends, and even in their enemies' lives.   They get it. They have eyes to see how great our God is and relentlessly pursue a relationship with Him.

Then there is the individual who attends church dutifully singing hymns without engaging their hearts. They speak lip service prayers and place gifts in the offering plate, gifts without worship, not giving the very best to Him.   Respectfully they listen to the message of God's Word, the praises, and prayers, but leave unchanged, unchallenged, untouched, unmoved, and unaffected. They leave the sanctuary with little regard for God. "It's the same, ole same ole."

Today, ask God to open our eyes and our ears.

North Clear Creek Falls, South of Lake City

Health Fair

Nevertheless, I will bring health and healing to it; I will heal my people and will let them enjoy abundant peace and security. Jeremiah 33:6 (NIV)

This morning was another blessing of living up here; the annual Lake City health fair and I saw Dr. Durmon, Laurie and Gudrun. Ever so thankfully I am not at the doctor's office often, it is always stressful for me but these kind souls make the event as pleasant as possible. My husband and I are all about preventive medicine so I made us the first appointments as soon as time slots were being scheduled.

Life is stressful enough with what is out of our control. We can help to manage a lot of our own healthfulness with preventive care.

What a blessing this amazing facility is for us Lake City folks! Thank you, Thank you to all the kind volunteers who help make this event possible.

Beloved, I wish above all things that thou mayest prosper and be in health, even as thy soul prospereth.
3 John 2 (KJV)

Alpine Gulch Trail

When he had heard therefore that he was sick, he abode two days still in the same place where he was. John 11:6 (KJV)

The Alpine Gulch Trail is a strenuous hike, but the scenic views are truly worth the effort. My daughter Kelly and I hiked it. We descended from the trailhead, crossed the bridge into a narrow canyon, hiking up the gulch, traversing the creek seven times, balancing on logs and slippery rocks. Then the trail climbs through aspen thickets, grassy meadows and spruce forests. The steep ascent leads to the Grassy Mountain Saddle. What spectacular views in every direction!

The trail connects to the Williams Creek Trail. We planned to make this connection and end our hike at the Williams Creek trailhead. However, on Grassy Mountain we lost the trail. We wandered. Finding a creek flowing down the mountainside, we decided to follow it, knowing it would take us to CR 30.

On this difficult descent, rocky and strewn with fallen branches, unexpectedly we spied a new born fawn in the creek. It shivered, lying in the clear, flowing water. Kelly and I delighted in the sight, admiring the beauty of new life and the frailty of the tiny creature. We surveyed our surroundings, looking for its mother knowing she must not be far away. We lingered a few more moments and continued down, leaving the fawn untouched.

Often, I think back to this incident. There is a Division of Wildlife flier that pictures a similar scene with the heading: "I haven't been abandoned."

There are times in life when we feel abandoned by God. Theologians label it "God's Silence." It is a time when we draw close to God and seek Him, but our prayers seemingly go unanswered. We feel numb, alone, forsaken, abandoned.

God's silence has a purpose. It is a sign that He is bringing you into an even more wonderful understanding of Himself, a new maturity. When you cannot hear God, He has trusted you in the most intimate way possible, a silence not of despair, but one of pleasure because He saw that you could endure an even bigger revelation.

If God has given you silence, then praise Him — He is bringing you into the mainstream of His purposes.

Patience

But our citizenship is in heaven. And we eagerly await a Savior from there, the Lord Jesus Christ.
Philippians 3:20 (NIV)

The snow is receding; the strong winds dry up the mud. Roads are graded and dust control applied. Parks are groomed. Windows are brought to a mirrored shine. Stores fronts are spruced-up and repaired; new inventory ordered and stocked; summer events scheduled and calendars printed. The annual Lake City Hinsdale County Vacation Guide is available along with the latest edition of the Silver Thread Scenic and Historic Byway Newspaper. Every business, every organization, county and town government, even individual families make preparation for summer and the tourist season.

And why not get ready for the promise of summer? We who live here wait in anticipation for visits from family, friends and acquaintances who now know someone that lives in paradise. Churches look forward to increased attendance. Retail shops, eating establishments, lodging facilities, town and county administrations and non-profits await the arrival of visitors from near and far. After all, ours is a tourist based economy.

We must prepare; we rely on this small window of opportunity, 4 to 6 months to earn a living, to gain needed dollars for upgrades, expansions and a host of "worthy" causes. We wonder if the sightseers and guests will come each year. Regardless, we make intensive preparation and look forward with anticipation.

Jesus Christ spoke often of His return to Earth. We do not have to wonder if He will return; He will come. Paul affirms that those who serve Christ, who are citizens of heaven are "eagerly awaiting for Him to return as our Savior." We are to be impatient for His return; expectantly preparing for His coming.

Like an excited 4-year old on Christmas Eve looking ahead to wished-for toys or like a lover longing for his beloved. Those who know Christ as Lord are to be anticipating His return with great desire. But also, we are to make preparation by living Godly lives, sharing the Gospel, prayer, and worship, and a daily, moment by moment relationship with Christ.

Ask yourself, "Am I eagerly waiting for my Jesus' return to Earth?" Why or why not? What needs to change in my life?"

On Growing Old

It is official; I am another year older as of this past Tuesday. After the events of this past month I told my immediate Beebe family that I am now the oldest, the matriarch, "the Queen Beebe if you please". They all got a kick out of that. I even got a birthday email asking if I was wearing my tiara.

A quote from Bette Davis, "Growing old isn't for sissies." I agree. I don't mind being old, but I do mind the sagging skin, dragging energy, and failing memory. I work on all of these, but to no avail. I am aging against my will. The alternative actually sounds great, "to be absent from the body is to be present with Christ." But I will have to await my numbered days.

What does the Bible have to say on the subject of growing older? Ecclesiastes 12:1-7 describes old age: when we get older our hands will tremble, our legs and back stoop, our teeth will fall out, our ears and eyes fail. It's not a pretty picture.

God says "Young people, it's wonderful to be young! Do everything you want to do; take it all in. But remember that you must give an account to God for everything you do." (11:9). don't let the excitement of youth cause you to forget your Creator. Honor him in your youth before you grow old and say, 'life isn't pleasant anymore.' Old people must give an account to God also.

Every life consists of "joys" and "yucks"; Good times and bad times; times of plenty and times of leanness; happiness and sorrow; moments that take your breath away and moments that knock the breath out of you. That is LIFE. Life is tough. Jesus says, "Here on earth you will have many trials and sorrows. But take heart, because I have overcome the world", John 16:33. Knowing this we need now to live for God. If you give your life to God and make him Lord and Master as well as Savior, put him first then life's "yucks" won't make you a bitter, grumpy "old person." Life between now and then will be tough, but if you live your life for Christ everyday from now until you are old then when you reflect on life you'll have plenty of great memories and an assured future.

If you're still young start living for God today and you'll be happy when you are older. If you are one of the elderly then remember that there is still a place in the church for you. If you don't have great memories to draw on because you didn't follow Christ at a young age then start now. It's never too late.

Retirement

As yet I am as strong this day as I was in the day that Moses sent me: as my strength was then, even so is my strength now, for war, both to go out, and to come in. Joshua 14:11

In checking census data it is noted 16.6% of the population is 65 or over; if you include 50 and over that percentage triples.Hinsdale County attracts retirees, and why not, with all the natural beauty, the relaxed living, and yet plenty of activities and volunteer opportunities to make the right mix. There are quality medical, public health services and a flourishing senior population.

Aging and slowing down should not be used in the same breath. Caleb is a wonderful example of an 85 year old who had lots of life to live.

When he was 40 years old, he was given a mission to explore the Promise Land (Numbers 13). He reported to the nation that God would give them the land, but the people rejected the good report. It cost them decades of heartache and wandering in the wilderness.

This is why his words in Joshua 14:11 are so poignant; 45 years later he is still on the mission God gave him so many years before.What is the secret of finishing well? It is serving God with a whole heart (Joshua 14:8, 9, 14). Caleb made this his lifetime priority, to follow the Lord wholeheartedly. That means that he followed God with unreserved enthusiasm, passion and commitment.

God recognized Caleb's devotion and Joshua confirmed it in granting his request for his inheritance.

Growing older has its challenges. But the key to making the most of whatever time God gives you is to find and lock in on your mission from God and never let go.

Each day, following the Lord should be a priority. How will you do that today and show your commitment with enthusiasm and passion?

Crystal Peak — Lake City

The Balloon Festival

The Lake City hot air balloon festival is an annual, much planned for, event in February. Plan as one might, the final say comes from the weather. As I write, the event this year was canceled and last year only one balloon got up and down quickly and safely before the winds became too strong for the delicate hot air balloons which could, only then be ridden, tethered.

What? A hot air balloon ride — tethered?

Too often we want to micro-manage God...let us have rain at this time and not at this time...I really, really want to have things turn out THIS WAY God...we need snow but these dates aren't a good time for it...this is a BAD situation God and people have free will but I am asking for your help...God Almighty is in control and though we might fuss about letting go, we are safer tethered with God. It is not a contradiction to be free in God while being tethered to God.

The name of the LORD is a strong tower; the righteous run to it and are safe. Proverbs: 18:10 (NIV)

Fourth of July—Religious Freedom

Fourth of July in Lake City — the parade, games in the park, street dance, fireworks, visiting with the towns many guests, and hamburgers and homemade ice cream at Bill and Elaine Nicholson's. But a more important part of our celebration is the Community Worship Service.

Amendment 1 — Congress shall make no law respecting an establishment of religion, or prohibiting the free exercise thereof; or abridging the freedom of speech, or of the press; or the right of the people peaceably to assemble, and to petition the Government for a redress.

The First Amendment is the single most important part of the Constitution. It protects the most basic human rights, the ability to speak one's mind. Sometimes I don't like it, but then I think of the alternative of being too frightened by possible consequences to actually do so. A free press keeps tabs on government activities and actions. How objective would a reporter be when his life is on the line because of his reporting?

Religious liberty has been called America's "first liberty" because freedom of the mind is logically and philosophically prior to all other freedoms protected by the Constitution. Freedom of religion is a key part of the boldest and most successful experiment in freedom the world has known. The strength and diversity of religion in the United States is due entirely to the full protection guaranteed by the Constitution.This means liberty for people of all faiths and NONE. I wish everyone had a personal saving relationship with Jesus. But each human has a free will. This is God's way.

However in regards to "free speech, freedom of religion, and a free press" I wonder why we Christians are so timid in proclaiming our faith, after all we believe Jesus is the "only way" to God. Are we afraid to "boldly" proclaim THE TRUTH? Have we "blended" into our culture, known for our tolerance? Is it a loss of our first love? Maybe it is a combination of all these.

Being "pushy" with our faith is not the way of grace. But if we do not exercise our freedom of religion, one of these days we might lose it or even worse stand before Christ as the man with the buried talent.

Flags of Freedom Wave — July 4th parade, Lake City

Extreme Makeover—Part 1

As a kid I used to see cartons in magazines where a big bully kicked sand in a scrawny runts face. Then the tiny guy would send off for the Charles Atlas body building program. The next thing you saw was the little runt had become a muscle man.Talk about an extreme makeover. And what woman hasn't seen the makeovers done in magazines where a dowdy "Plain Jane" becomes a "Beautiful Betty?"

What is it about these makeovers that are so appealing? Is it the thought that anyone can become stronger, better, smarter, more beautiful? Or is it that we are not satisfied with who and what we are? Perhaps it is a little of both.

Each one of us is uniquely who we are not through the roll of the genetic dice but through the sovereign design of the omnipotent creator Father God. Each one of us is made in His image with our own distinct DNA, personality traits; even in the family He placed us in and time in history. But alas, we are not perfect in the sense that our bodies are temporary and we are bent toward evil and we exist in a world that is cursed because it is ruled by the prince of the power of the air. No wonder we crave for an extreme makeover.

But God knows that and has already provided for OUR EXTREME MAKEOVER.

We are given a NEW HEART and a NEW SPIRIT. Ezekiel 36:26 says, "I will give you a NEW HEART and put a NEW SPIRIT within you; and I will remove the heart of stone from your flesh and give you a heart of flesh."

God gives us a NEW MIND (Don't we all need that?). Hebrews 8:10 quotes from the Old Testament, "I will put My laws into their MINDS, and I will write them on their hearts." And 1 Corinthians 2:16, "But we have the MIND OF CHRIST." And Romans 12:2,"..but be TRANSFORMED by the RENEWING of you MIND".

Our Father gives us a NEW NATURE, 2 Corinthians 5:17, "Therefore if anyone is in Christ, he is a NEW CREATURE; the old things passed away; behold, new things have come." METAMORPHOSIS is the Greek word here; caterpillar to butterfly.

This makeover is taking place moment by moment as we serve and love Him.

Extreme Makeover—Part 2

But God has even more changes in store for us...

We are going to get a NEW BODY (Yea!) 1 Corinthians 15:53, "For this perishable must put on the imperishable, and this mortal must put on immortality." 1 John 3:2, "We know that when He (Jesus) appears, we will be like Him..." a glorified, perfect body!

And lastly we are given a NEW NAME. Revelation 2:17, 'And I will give him a white stone and a NEW NAME written on the stone..." To complete our makeover we are given a new name that embodies the NEW person that we have become.

Lake San Cristobal

Simple pleasures

A friend in a metroplex emailed: "today while I was driving I found a Christian music station and it was great to drive with that playing."

While walking the dogs in the snow today, I was conscious of the clean, crisp mountain air.

Desperately today, needing to laugh with an understanding girlfriend, and she came through when I phoned.

Again today I told my loving husband that I am proud to be his wife.

A friend did a totally unexpected and unnecessary kindness.

"Our life is frittered away by detail. Simplify, simplify, simplify! I say, let your affairs be as two or three, and not a hundred or a thousand; instead of a million count half a dozen, and keep your accounts on your thumbnail." Henry David Thoreau

Leanin' Trees

I pray that out of his glorious riches he may strengthen you with power through his Spirit in your inner being, so that Christ may dwell in your hearts through faith. And I pray that you, being rooted and established in love, Ephesians 3:16-17 (NIV)

Leanin' Tree greeting cards have been around since the company's humble beginning in 1949 when two men strapped for cash traded art for advertising. The Boulder based business has grown from four western Christmas cards to offer over 3,000 unique greeting cards in a multitude of themes for everyday occasions and major holidays. Long before moving to Lake City, when looking for a distinctive card, I would search for Leanin' Tree designs. However, the company's name was a mystery. I was acquainted with fallen trees, but never a "leaning" tree.

The area around Lake City presents many glimpses of leaning trees, along the banks of Henson Creek the lower path of the Slumgullion Earth Flow and the Lake Fork of the Gunnison River. Leaning is a structural weakness and is a clue to the potential of impending tree failure. Shallow roots, roots exposed by soil erosion, root diseases and severed roots, lie as the major cause of leaning.

Similarly we can be like leaning trees. We have "root" issues. Shallow roots are the result of not spending time in God's Word or with God's people, or not developing a close relationship with Christ in prayer. There are times that roots are exposed through erosion, exposure to our culture and its influence. Severed roots occur when we intentionally distance ourselves from God, his "nudging", His Word, and His church.

Paul writes to the Church at Ephesus, confirming his prayer for each individual, that Christ has unlimited resources available and can empower them with inner strength, by the power of the Holy Spirit. He then reveals the secret to healthy roots: letting Christ make his home in your heart and trusting him. It is only then that your roots will grow down in God's love, establishing and making you strong.

Examine your heart. How strong are your roots in Christ Jesus? Adversity, life's storms and individuals, can reveal how shallow or how deep, how diseased or healthy, our true relationship with Christ.

Kindness

Departing Mountains and God's Everlasting Kindness

Though the mountains be shaken and the hills be removed, yet my unfailing love for you will not be shaken nor my covenant of peace be removed," says the LORD, who has compassion on you.
Isaiah 54:10 (NIV)

The sight of mountains takes my breath away. The first time I saw them up close and personal was on senior trip — the Smoky Mountains of Tennessee. What a spectacular vision, awesome in beauty! I drank in the view. I memorized each horizon, the clear running streams.

No less inspiring was my first glimpse of the Rockies. I recall stopping in Lincoln County, New Mexico and telling the visitor center worker my thoughts of those mountains. She told me they were "foothills, wait till you see the mammoth peaks of Colorado." She was right. After fifteen years of being surrounded by precipice after precipice, bluffs, cliffs and crags, it still takes my breath away! The mountains are comforting to me, with their stability and immobility. They are so substantial and strong, Herculean and ageless.

Then I read Isaiah 54:10, "mountains depart." What does that mean? One translation says "shaken" but most versions use the word "depart" or "removed."

The mountains seem so solid and secure. The fact is that created things pass away, even when it appears that they are unchanging. The emphasis is on the eternal, faithful, trustworthy, dependable, constant, steadfast, and reliable. That is the *kindness* of God. God's kindness is *eternal.*

Humans often forget this. We sing "God is good," but then leave church and begin to focus on everything that is going bad in our lives. The kids are driving us crazy. My mate is mean, unfaithful. I can't pay the bills. We need rain. Business is bad. I lost my job. I hurt. I have cancer. I am growing old. We obsess about the things that "come to pass." God's kindnesses, compassion, love, mercy, grace, care for you and carefulness with you are everlasting.

Yes, many times, the circumstances of life are bad. But God's kindness is ALWAYS — even in the midst of horrendous situations. His kindness will not go away. Today make an effort to let your mind dwell on the kindness of God.

The Golden Rule

"...thou shalt love thy neighbor as thyself.",
Leviticus 19:18

Living by the Golden Rule would make us better people living in a happier community.

Practicing empathy and compassion is a good place to start. Trying to understand what another person is going through and finding little ways to make their day more joyful only takes a bit of time and thoughtfulness. Everyone wants to feel like someone cares about them. Most people respond to kindness.

Being helpful is a choice. Sadly there is a tendency to keep to oneself, and to ignore the problems of others. Don't be blind to the needs and troubles of others. Look to help even before asked. You may be proud of your independence and just expect others to take care of their own needs as well, but life is constantly changing. You may need help in ways you never anticipated. The way you treat others will come back to you.

We all want to talk. We all want to be heard, but really listening to others, taking the time to actually listen to another person, rather than just waiting to talk, takes skill and practice. Listening helps us understand one another.

No one likes to be criticized and controlled by others. Children too, deserve to be treated with the Golden Rule.

Too often people have a tendency to strike back when treated badly. The Golden Rule isn't about retaliation, smile and try to stay away from or limit time around mean-spirited people. Those kinds of people teach us how not to be in our dealings with others.

Lake City has CCS, Christian Community Service. This organization is like a neighbor helping a neighbor. CCS is designed to help local folks 'get back on their feet.' It is designed as a short-term assistance program. Funds come from the offerings taken up at the 4th of July and Easter community church services and of course CCS donations are welcomed at all times.

Gandhi told us to be the change we want to see in the world. Wouldn't it be great to see people treating each other with more compassion and kindness! Let it begin with me!

Living in Bear Country

The LORD is near to all who call on him, to all who call on him in truth. He fulfills the desires of those who fear him; he hears their cry and saves them.
Psalm 145:18-19 (NIV)

The San Juan Mountains are native habitat for the Black Bear. Today bears are sharing space with the population of Lake City. Evidence of their presence is observed by the damage to trash dumpsters and strewn garbage. Bears are sited ambling along Gunnison Avenue, in front of the medical center, and on my back porch.

There is lots of information on living and vacationing in Bear County, practical guidelines to help us do our part to prevent human-bear conflicts. However, bears are curious, intelligent, and very resourceful and will explore possible food sources. If they find food near homes, campgrounds, vehicles, or communities they will return for more.

Julie called me, distraught because of a big Black Bear near her home. Her dogs were barking crazily, the bear inquisitive, longingly gazing at her and her home. "Who do I call?" She inquired. She called a neighbor who nonchalantly responded, "No big deal." The sheriff's office referred her to the Department of Wildlife. The DOW rehearsed a well known list of rules. Rules were obeyed and the bear was still there on her property, causing fear and dread for both her and her dogs.

That is when she was told by the Department of Wildlife, "Deal with it!"

Fear. Crisis. The unknown. Sickness. Rejection. Deception. Death. Something bigger than we are. We turn to those who should be there to help us and yet we find no aid, no answers, and no comfort. Sometimes they cannot be reached by telephone or email. Friends, family, banks, organizations, government, or whomever we have confidence in frequently will not or cannot help or are helpless to help. At times human help is worthless.

BUT GOD, who is always present, tells us to CALL on Him. He reassures us that he hears us and WILL SAVE US. Repeatedly in His Word his people are told to call on Him when they are in trouble and He will answer, help, deliver, defend, and comfort. When we are in trouble, whatever the need, He is the answer. He never ignores our problem. He is a father who cares about his sons and daughters; their names are "engraved" on his hands. He is "a very present help in time of trouble."

We never have to "just deal with it."

Friends of the Bears

It is more than a necessary kindness to take care of the bears by keeping them wild, by keeping our distance and all traces of food as far away as is possible as we live in the wild animal's domain. It is another reminder of how our actions with our environment have consequences and of our responsibilities to the animals, both wild and domestic.

Calling my dear friend to check on her after yesterday's operation I learned that she and her daughter had just returned from the animal clinic. After weeks of struggling with herself her daughter finally followed the tender, caring advice of her veterinarian and loved ones and put her darling little dog down.

Our beloved pets give us joy and depend on us for everything. "To everything there is a season." Ecclesiastes 3:1~ there is a time for everything, and a season for every activity under the heavens: a time to be born and a time to die...

God made the animals and God made us, knowing the bond that most of us would have with animals. It is fitting that we celebrate Francis of Assisi.

This past October we were all together at St. James with our beloved pets celebrating the Feast Day of St. Francis, who is fondly remembered for loving the animals.

It has been said that Francis could communicate with the animals and that he felt as one with all creation.

As we live in the midst of nature we need to improve on how to do that gently as not to destroy the reason we choose to live here in the first place.

Part of that practice includes living in bear country.

Lake City Friends of the Bears is dedicated to the reduction of bear-human conflict through many educational projects and the use of humane bear deterrents.

Annuals and Perennials

But the fruit of the Spirit is love, joy, peace, long suffering, gentleness, goodness, faith, Meekness, temperance: against such there is no law.
Galatians 5:22-23

At Lake City's high altitude planting time comes when freezing temperatures are past, normally about the middle of June It is a time for working in flower beds, digging in dirt, pulling the remnants of the previous year's blooms, adding new soil and fertilizer. And it is the time to plant flowers. A decision must be made....annuals or perennials?

An annual plant blooms only once in an annual cycle. You plant a seed or seedling plant, it grows foliage, flowers, seeds and the plant dies all in the same year. Annual flowers tend to bloom from spring until autumn frost. Though they must be replanted each year, annuals are hard to beat in terms of bright, showy, season-long color.

Perennial flowers are those that grow for three or more years. Sometimes a perennial may not be mature enough to bloom the first year from seed. Perennials will need periodic rejuvenation. Most perennials bloom for only a short period.

As I pondered the decision, which is not so difficult; perennials give more "bang for the buck."

But then I think, "I want flowers ALL SEASON LONG."

It seems to me the fruit of the spirit is manifest like annuals and perennials. Sometimes it is so easy to love others, especially when we have things in common or are only with them once a week. I can be patient, with those I love and kindness to those who are kind to me. That's a breeze. These fruit are like the annuals, showy, effortless and pretty much unproblematic.

But what if I work with a jerk? Self-control must be perennial, coming from my relationship with Christ. Someone races around me when I am driving in the speed limit; kindness can be hard. I pray and God seemingly has turned away. Faith must be lasting. Gloom because of the economy, joy can be persistent, like the perennials that continue in all seasons. Sometimes they are apparent but even when they are not seen, they are still present.

Annuals or perennials? No need to pick one or the other. Annuals and perennials can be combined to reap the best of both. The same is true with the fruit of the spirit. Both come from abiding in Christ and both make for the character of Christ.

Above My Computer Part 1

ANYWAY
People are unreasonable, illogical, and self-centered,
LOVE THEM ANYWAY
If you do good, people will accuse you of selfish,
ulterior motives,
DO GOOD ANYWAY
If you are successful, you win false friends and true enemies,
SUCCEED ANYWAY
The good you do will be forgotten tomorrow,
DO GOOD ANYWAY
Honesty and frankness make you vulnerable,
BE HONEST AND FRANK ANYWAY
What you spent years building,
may be destroyed overnight,
BUILD ANYWAY
People really need help,
but may attack you if you help them,
HELP PEOPLE ANYWAY
Give the world the best you have
and you'll get kicked in the teeth,
GIVE THE WORLD THE BEST YOU'VE GOT ANYWAY.
from Mother Teresa's wall

Though attributed to Mother Teresa, I have learned that the poem known as The Paradoxical Commandments were written by Kent M. Keith at 19, as part of a book for student leaders entitled *The Silent Revolution: Dynamic Leadership in the Student Council,* published in 1968.

"I saw a lot of idealistic young people go out into the world to do what they thought was right, and good, and true, only to come back a short time later, discouraged, or embittered, because they got negative feedback, or nobody appreciated them, or they failed to get the results they had hoped for." recalls Keith. "I told them that if they were going to change the world, they had to really love people, and if they did, that love would sustain them. I also told them that they couldn't be in it for fame or glory. I said that if they did what was right and good and true, they would find meaning and satisfaction, and that meaning and satisfaction would be enough."

The Paradoxical Commandments were part of a chapter entitled "Brotherly What?": "I laid down the Paradoxical Commandments as a challenge," Keith said. "The challenge is to always do what is right and good and true, even if others don't appreciate it. You have to keep striving, no matter what, because if you don't, many of the things that need to be done in our world will never get done."

Christ came to a world filled with people who were unreasonable, illogical, and self-centered, yet He loved them anyway. He did everything well and was accused of selfish, ulterior motives, but He did good anyway. In giving His best He suffered rejection, shame, false accusations, and death.

Yet He gave His best ANYWAY.

You and I can do no less.

Above My Computer Part 2: A Starfish

Attending a "Build a Generation" meeting, Tara, the Youth Services Coordinator, ended her presentation with the following story:

A young girl was walking along a beach upon which thousands of starfish had been washed up during a terrible storm. When she came to each starfish, she would pick it up, and throw it back into the ocean. People watched her with amusement.

She had been doing this for some time when a man approached her and said, "Little girl, why are you doing this? Look at this beach! You can't save all these starfish. You can't begin to make a difference!" The girl seemed crushed, suddenly deflated. But after a few moments, she bent down, picked up another starfish, and hurled it as far as she could into the ocean. Then she looked up at the man and replied, "Well, I made a difference to that one!"

The old man looked at the girl inquisitively and thought about what she had done and said. Inspired, he joined the little girl in throwing starfish back into the sea. Soon others joined, and all the starfish were saved". - adapted from the Star Thrower by Loren C. Eiseley.

Tara then gave each person there a sponge starfish. Mine is purple and today, ten years later it hangs on my bulletin board as a reminder that it only takes one person to make a difference in someone's life. It does not take a lot of money, a big organization, or even a detailed plan. It is one person, giving of themselves to another.

At one time I was like that starfish and one person believed in me and made all the difference in the world. Now, that is my desire, to make a difference in someone's life, one person at a time.

I tell you that in the same way there will be more rejoicing in heaven over one sinner who repents than over ninety-nine righteous persons who do not need to repent. Luke 15:7 (NIV)

Sheep Day on Engineer Pass.

Goodness

Called to be Heroes

I love Christmas movies. I can watch one right after the other for hours. I like the "feel good" sentiment they give me and that everyone lives "happily ever after" even though I know that is not reality. "White Christmas", "It's a Wonderful Life", "Miracle on 34th Street" are classics I try to see every year. But another favorite is "Die Hard." (The edited version) Christmas is not complete if I can't watch "Die Hard." "Ho, Ho, Ho, now I have a machine gun."

It's a great Christmas movie. The plot is about a New York cop who has come at Christmas to see his estranged wife and kids. At her work place, while he is alone waiting for his wife, thieves posing as terrorists take the partying workers hostage. These evil guys kill indiscriminately while their computer whiz is working to open the safe to steal a fortune in bearer bonds.

John, the policeman sees what is happening and tries desperately to get help, but all to no avail. Instead he is a one man army that single handily foils the crooks plans, saves the hostages and loot and rides away with his cherished wife.

How does this relate to the Christmas story? Jesus came as a vulnerable baby in a manger, a lone alien invader coming to earth to see his estranged bride, be reconciled to lost Israel and the Gentiles. Our movie hero loves his wife and wants reconciliation.

Unlike our hero, Jesus knows that the adversary is here to "steal, kill, and destroy." He is not taken by surprise. Both men, John and Jesus know the enemy must be defeated. The movie is bloody. So is the Christmas Story. Often we breeze over the fact that Herod killed thousands of innocent baby boys.

Jesus is alone; there is no cavalry to assist him. Yes he has trained the disciples, but what a miserable lot they proved to be for Him — betrayed, denied, and forsaken.

But in the end good triumphs over evil, Jesus the lone underdog triumphs over the enemy. Underdog? How inconceivable that one lone baby who becomes one lone man could defeat such a powerful, scheming enemy? What else would you call one human pitted against principalities and powers and wickedness in high places as well at the dragon himself? But that is exactly what Jesus did — defeated the adversary of man and God.

Fuzzy, feel-good movies are not what Christmas is about. It is about Satan's defeat.

A Declaration Of Independence

I am the vine, ye are the branches: He that abideth in me, and I in him, the same bringeth forth much fruit: for without me ye can do nothing.
John 15:5

Thomas Jefferson wrote of the Declaration of Independence that the document did not aim at originality of principle or sentiment, but was intended to be an expression of the American mind.

Times have changed since Jefferson penned "We hold these truths to be self-evident, that all men are created equal, that they are endowed by their Creator with certain unalienable rights that among these are life, liberty and the pursuit of happiness." Today many Americans do not believe in "their Creator." Life is not an "unalienable right" it is terminated daily by abortion, murder, and euthanasia. Liberty and the Bill of Rights are slowly being chipped away. The pursuit of happiness however is alive and well.

What did Jefferson mean "an expression of the American mind?" I believe he was referring to the desire for independence and individuality, not to be con- trolled by others in matters of opinion, conduct, and the capacity for each human to choose their own path. Even in the acknowledgment of the need of government the framers of the Constitution recognized it was not about control, but "to establish justice, insure domestic tranquility, provide for the common defense, promote the general welfare, and secure the blessings of liberty."

Independence and individuality are reliance on self. I love my independence and prize my individuality, though these are only an illusion. I think I can survive on my own, make my own way, support myself, think for myself, plan my future and control my destiny. However, the Bible is clear. Jesus said, "Without me you can do nothing." My heart beats because of the grace of God. For it is in Him that we live and move and have our being.

But there is an area we each control and are truly independent. Each us has a will. God never wanted puppets, but beings that would by individual, independent choice , choose to love Him. Each man, woman, boy and girl has this truly "unalienable" right. By telling God you want your independence and individuality, one has chosen slavery to the taskmasters of Satan, Sin, and Self.

Will it be freedom or slavery? Heaven or hell? Life or Death? It is an individual choice no one can make for another person. Will you declare your independence by choosing God?

Perfect Goodness

What shall we then say to these things? If God be for us, who can be against us? He that spared not his own Son, but delivered him up for us all, how shall he not with him also freely give us all things?
Romans 8:31-32

Pretty powerful stuff! If God is for us, who can be against us? I heard Pastor David Beebe, of the Lake City First Baptist Church, give a sermon once that included the truth that none of us have to make this life's journey alone.

God is with us! Living in this mountain community that is especially evident with the churches, events, volunteer opportunities and gathering places so numerous for a town this size. Read the Silver World, attend church services, community gatherings and pick your opportunity. The Bible says:

And everyone who calls on the name of the Lord will be saved. Acts 2:21 (NIV)

Fear not, little flock; for it is your Father's good pleasure to give you the kingdom. Luke 12:32

The Bible does not say if you follow this particular doctrine you will be saved. Religions are tools that "should" help us get closer to God. Religions are made by flawed people, "for all have sinned and fall short of the glory of God." Therefore, we must be careful we are not following or infatuated with, imperfect, human beings, but that we are praising, trusting and following Christ.

For God is: omniscience (infinite knowledge), omnipotent (unlimited power), omnipresent (present everywhere) and omnibenevolent (perfect goodness). God is perfect Love.

"We know that God is everywhere; but certainly we feel His presence most when His works are on the grandest scale spread before us; and it is in the unclouded night-sky, where His worlds wheel their silent course, that we read clearest His infinitude, His omnipotence, His omnipresence." from Jane Eyre by Charlotte Brontë

Goodness in a Long Winter Rest

A solstice is the astronomical event that occurs twice each year as the sun reaches its highest or lowest point in the sky.

Our winter solstice, the shortest day of the year, is usually on December 21st or 22nd each year.

It was you who set all the boundaries of the earth; you made both summer and winter.
Psalm 74:17 (NIV)

We locals talk about the lack of daylight about as much as we talk about the snow or the lack of snow. Some of us, the same people who stay up until 11pm summer nights are in bed by 8:30 these cold winter nights. Both animals and humans are touched by the love of God that reaches down and tucks us in early on these dark, cold, winter nights, knowing of the activity to come in the summer. There is goodness in a long winter's rest.

Thou art my hiding place; thou shalt preserve me from trouble; thou shalt compass me about with songs of deliverance. Selah. Psalm 32:7 (KJV)

Slowing Down

Dogs are good company and great for making us do what is better for us: getting up from working on the computer and going on a walk.

Truthfully, my heart and mind were not on the walk, I wanted to be back working on the computer. I let the three year-old, Joy, lead and then pulled Spring, the nine-year-old, along behind.

A cold current of air started blowing, storm clouds were on the horizon and while it was mid-May, I shivered though my layers which ended with my down vest.

Trying to hurry our dog Spring on the path along Henson Creek was like trying to hurry the spring season in Lake City; it's not gonna happen.

As I sighed and waited, I noticed little white flowers that looked like snowflakes on a stem, which had been there all along. I smiled and felt some stress leave my shoulders. Spring, our dog, looked up grateful that I had stopped pulling. Spring, the season, was smiling too.

Volunteering

Lewis Carroll wrote, "All that is really worth the doing is what we do for others." Robert Louis Stevenson wrote, "The world is so full of a number of things, I'm sure we should all be as happy as kings."

The world is filled with opportunities to do an infinite number of things to make a difference when we align our efforts with the activities that speak to our soul. It is so easy to be negative, but doing something to grow more positive is better! As we acknowledge we are a 'work in progress' and work on ourselves instead of just complaining about our weight, our work place or our relationships, we need to thank God for the amazing miracles of our bodies! We need to thank God for work! We need to thank God for the people in our lives!

By the miracle of being born in the United States of America, we live amazing blessed and protected lives. While laws and politicians are not perfect, our basic human rights and civil liberties are protected. As a work in progress, we need constant reminding to vote, to appreciate and to work.

By the miracle of living in the mountains, be it for the rest of our lives, or for a day, or somewhere in between, we live in the midst of daily miracles. This moment is an amazing wonder! Right now is a phenomenon! In this exquisite area, these picturesque mountains do not change from the grandest house to the most modest. If I choose to be here because I love the mountains, then all I need to do is breathe the sweet air and be blessed.

Volunteering in Lake City is as natural to hard working, creative folks as is breathing the sweet mountain air. It is a great way to meet people and be a blessing. Lake City has many different organizations that are always in need of volunteers.

St. James Episcopal Church — Lake City

Whitmore Falls - Soaking in God

My heart says of you, "Seek his face!" Your face, LORD, I will seek. Psalm 27:8 (NIV)

Unseen from County Road 20 is Whitmore Falls. The falls seems to be beneath the road and drops into a stunning pool before the water continues its journey down Henson Creek to Lake City.

Taking the trail leads to a safe viewing platform. Before the construction of the present trail, a not so well marked path led to the foot of the falls. It was steep and strewn with loose rocks. Our 10-year-old grandson and a companion were visiting and we decided to make the trek down to the bottom of Whitmore Falls. Boys love this kind of thing and I still had the knees to do it.

Upon arrival at our quest, we sat and ate our picnic lunch. Then the boys waded into the pristine pool. Despite of the chilliness of the water this quickly became a time for a swim. I laid back on the rock, listening to the laughter of boys in play, enjoying the warmth of the sun and the moist spray on my face. I was savoring the moment, soaking it in, and etching it in my memory and on my heart.

Savoring God and Soaking Him in — I never thought about these terms in relationship to God, but then someone invited me to a time of "soaking." Immediately, I knew what she was talking about; sitting in the presence of God seeking Him.

Not asking for anything, not petitioning or whining, or pleading on the behalf of others, but simply savoring his presence, soaking Him in; focusing on who God is; His character, His works, His ways.

Psalm 46:10, "*Be still and know that I am God.*" Be still literally means to cease from striving. Go, relax, tune out the world and listen to the quiet whisper of God. Not always easy in our "connected" world of technology. But the invitation and call is the same, get still and come into a place of rest, soak in the presence of God. Then you will know that He is God.

The word 'know' means to know by experience. It is not being still and knowing ABOUT God. It is being still and KNOWING God by being in his presence, savoring God, soaking Him in; focusing our heart, spirit, soul, mind, and body on Him.

Take time, right this moment get still, invite His presence, and seek His face. He will show up.

River Access Trail

Rivers of Living Water

In the last day, that great day of the feast, Jesus stood and cried, saying, If any man thirst, let him come unto me, and drink. He that believeth on me, as the scripture hath said, out of his belly shall flow rivers of living water. (But this spake he of the Spirit, which they that believe on him should receive: for the Holy Ghost was not yet given; because that Jesus was not yet glorified.) John 7:37-39

Coming from the south as you cross the Henson Creek Pedestrian bridge there is a sign, "River Access Trail." The trail is a short loop, beginning at the bridge, includes a boardwalk with view of the confluence of the Henson Creek and Lake Fork of the Gunnison River. Though the walk is only 1170 feet it is part of a larger trail system that includes the Lake Fork Trail around Memorial Park, Nature Access Trail, the Lake Fork Trail and the Henson Creek Trail that runs west along 1st Street until it intersects Henson Creek Road and ends at the ATV staging area.

"River Access"—the words simply mean I have a right of way to the river, a right to use the river, an entrance in, and have contact with the river. Those who walk these trails have access to the water; they can fish in it, wade in it, or even swim. The walker may simply glimpse or gaze at the river or pay no attention at all to the water but rather be intent on their thoughts and completing an exercise program.

"Anyone who believes in me (Jesus) MAY come and drink!" There is a choice involved. One may believe, but never drink.

There are two experiences, one is the new birth when a sinner comes to Christ for forgiveness of sins and receives Him into his heart. This is a well of water, springing up into everlasting life. The other, the infilling of the Holy Spirit, is rivers. Not just one river, but rivers. The water in the well (salvation) is for one purpose: it blesses you. It is for your benefit. But the rivers, the infilling of the Holy Spirit, flow out of you to bless someone else.

The purpose of being filled with the Holy Spirit is so that you might be a blessing to others. Some people say, "If you are born of the Spirit, you have the Spirit, and that's all there is to it." But, no, just because you've had one drink of water is no sign that you are full of water.

As a follower of Christ you have ACCESS to rivers of living water. Will you be one that out of your belly will flow rivers of living water?

Pentecost Sunday

Pentecost was originally an Old Testament festival calculated as beginning on the fiftieth day after the beginning of Passover. In the Christian calendar, it falls on the seventh Sunday after Easter.

Christians commemorate Pentecost as the descent of the Holy Spirit upon the Apostles and other followers of Jesus as described in Acts 2:1-31. Pentecost is sometimes described as the "Birthday of the Church". The term Pentecost is used 3 times in the New Testament: Acts 2:1, Acts 20:16, and 1 Corinthians 16:8.

The narrative of Pentecost is in Acts 2:1-6 *"And when the day of Pentecost was fully come, they were all with one accord in one place. And suddenly there came a sound from heaven as of a rushing mighty wind, and it filled all the house where they were sitting. And there appeared unto them cloven tongues like as of fire, and it sat upon each of them. And they were all filled with the Holy Ghost, and began to speak with other tongues, as the Spirit gave them utterance."*

Many people were confounded. Then Peter with the eleven proclaimed to the crowd that this event was the fulfillment of the prophecy. *I will pour out my spirit.* Joel 2:28-29 and Acts 2:41 reports: *Then they that gladly received his word were baptized: and the same day there were added unto them about three thousand souls.*

So why is Pentecost important to us the church? Are the events of Acts 2 repeatable in this 21st century?

Should it or should it not become a paradigm for personal religious experience?   I speak in tongues and believe it is important for the church today. But Pentecost is not only about speaking in a prayer language.Pentecost represents God's gracious, enabling presence, actively at work among His people, giving them power to live out in dynamic ways the witness of being His people.

It is about the power and person of the Holy Spirit taking up residence in the believer making it possible to do the impossible, empowerment to witness, to lay hands on the sick and they recover, and to cast out demons. In other words, the significance of Pentecost is the receiving of power to do the works of Christ. The true evidence of a personal "Pentecostal experience" is TO BE CHRIST LIKE, walking in his steps, performing his works, and proclaiming Him.

A Walk in The Clouds

Therefore, since we are surrounded by such a great cloud of witnesses, let us throw off everything that hinders and the sin that so easily entangles, and let us run with perseverance the race marked out for us. Let us fix our eyes on Jesus. Hebrews 12:1-2 (NIV)

Our cabin north of town sits on the rim of the Blue Mesa Subdivision overlooking a valley.The Lake City cut-off road is to the North West; we can see Mount Crested Butte and Monarch.However, there are mornings when dense fog fills the valley; we are looking over the tops of the clouds. At other times the thick moisture surrounds our home and visibility is reduced immensely. When it is like this I think that I am walking in the clouds.

Recently David and I awakened to just such a morning. The mist engulfed our home; we could feel the wetness of the cloud on our faces. I sat down to en- joy a cup of coffee and gaze at my own personal cloud. The words of Hebrews 12:1-2 came to mind; I am surrounded by a great cloud of witnesses. They are invisible, yet I know they are there.

In Hebrews, chapter 11, the writer lists a host of men and women who gained God's approval because of their faith. They understood that the things that are seen were not made of things that are visible. (11:2) They believed in an invisible God and a world of the invisible. These individuals lived with the invisible kingdom in mind. Why else would Abraham leave his home, his comfort zone, and his family?

How could Abraham even consider sacrificing his son Isaac? Moses rejected the fame, power, and riches of this life and endured "as seeing Him who is unseen." Rahab risks her life to save two strangers. All of these people mentioned received God's approval because of theirfaith, yet none received all that God had promised.God had far better things in mind that they could not receive until "you and I" finish the race.

Therefore — an important word — because these heroes of the faith serve as our fans, our own personal cheering squad that encourages and rejoices and sorrows with us.

Like that cloud in Blue Mesa that morning, this invisible host surrounds each one of us 24/7. Because of this, I must stop sinning and doing the things that would hinder me from living for Christ and focus on Him.

Most times we are unaware of the invisible that surrounds us. Ask God to reveal the invisible and live with the invisible kingdom in mind.

Rainbows

Whenever I bring clouds over the earth and the rainbow appears in the clouds, I will remember my covenant between me and you and all living creatures of every kind. Never again will the waters become a flood to destroy all life. Whenever the rainbow appears in the clouds, I will see it and remember the everlasting covenant. Genesis 9:14-16 (NIV)

In late summer and early fall, during the "monsoon" season, the skies over Lake City often display spectacular rainbows. Early one morning after a rain, I spied a double rainbow over the First Baptist Church. I had never seen this before and rushed to retrieve my camera to commemorate the occasion.

Isaac Newton, in 1665, first analyzed the technical details of rainbow formation. However, the scientific explanation does not diminish my pleasure and delight when I see a rainbow. It does not detract from the beauty and complexity of God's creation or His amazing promise.

In Genesis 6-9 there is a record of the wickedness of man. God was sorry that he had made man and He was grieved in his heart (6:6) and therefore planned to blot man from the face of the earth. This would be done by a flood that would cover the whole earth.

But, Noah found favor in the eyes of the Lord. (6:8) Given instructions by God, Noah built an ark, a three story boat; read the measurements in Genesis 6:14-16. God told him what to bring to the ark, his family, two each of every unclean animal and seven of every clean animal, male and female, and food for all.

After Noah obeyed, God shut the door and the earth and all that was in it was destroyed by water. After a year of being bombarded by the noise of animals, the ark rested on dry land and the eight humans and all the animals left the ark.

In gratitude Noah built an altar to the Lord and offered burnt offerings. And "The Lord smelled the soothing aroma" (8:21) and makes a vow to never destroy every living thing again and then gives the rainbow as a sign, a symbol of his promise.

Read the account in Genesis 6-9:17 and reflect on the trustworthiness of his promises.

Staying light longer

My husband and I live in a valley so in the winter that lack of direct sunlight is incredibly noticeable. Sunshine comes pouring into our windows about 8:30am and leaves about 2:30pm. The lack of sunlight in winter makes the house physically, as well as mentality, cold. Therefore, I absolutely notice when the sun is staying for bits of longer intervals.

It is warmer this morning, though at -12° it is still very cold of course. I take pleasure in the warm cozy comforts of my thick robe, a crackling fire and hot coffee. The blue sky and sunshine promise another spectacular day. I want to pass on the joy I feel with the promise of this new day!

Though paraphrased, parts of a song I enjoyed as a girl comes to mind: 'That's how it is with God's love, once you've experienced it, you'll spread His Love to everyone, you'll want to pass it on! I'll shout it from the mountain top…Praise God!...I want the world to know…the Lord of Love has come to me, I want to pass it on."

Unpretentiousness

Christ was born in a stable. That is significantly basic, quite simple.

Simplicity is a theme in Christianity. St. Thomas Aquinas said that God is infinitely simple. The Franciscans are all about simplicity. The Quakers practice the Testimony of Simplicity, which is the simplifying of one's life in order to focus on things that are most important and disregard or avoid things that are least important.

The largest professed religion in the United States is Christianity, yet Christianity and simplicity, at least in the United States, seems to be a contradiction.

Can we really have all the trappings of wealth and be as Christ teaches?

Can we really be as Christ and not have our vote, or our actions be to help those less prosperous?

Faithfulness

Planting Seeds

It is officially the middle of spring now, though we are still getting snow in late May, the mixture of moisture and sunshine is good for growing things. Tilling our garden soil is often rewarded with such a delight as to find minuscule plants growing from left over summer seeds.

Seeds are little miracles. Wikipedia states that the oldest viable carbon-14-dated seed that has grown into a plant was a Judean date palm seed about 2,000 years old, recovered from excavations at Herod the Great's palace on Masada in Israel. It was germinated in 2005.

Over the winter, Carol Lynn excitedly reports to our Lake City Pilates class, how the care she has been taking for her seeds is paying off and by the end of May the seedlings are for sale at the annual Lake City Health Fair, with the proceeds going to the community garden.

It's all a win-win situation where everyone can experience the joy of a little miracle, which began with a seed.

Let us not become weary in doing good, for at the proper time we will reap a harvest if we do not give up. Galatians 6:9 (NIV)

When you have eaten and are satisfied, praise the LORD your God for the good land he has given you.
Deuteronomy 8:10 (NIV)

Double waterfall at Nellie Creek

The Stinger Band

Neither yield ye your members as instruments of unrighteousness unto sin: but yield yourselves unto God, as those that are alive from the dead, and your members as instruments of righteousness unto God.
Romans 6:13

The first Lake City Brass and String bands were formed about 1877. Organized in 1878, the Pitkin Guards drum and bugle corps and brass band provided entertainment that added to the town's active social life by performing at dances, celebrations, and town ceremonies.

The current Lake City Stinger Band was formed in the spring of 1997 with Durell Thompson as director. Most band members are musicians that have retired their band instruments, but there are also novices, and even those who play no instrument, but are interested in music, all are invited to come be a part of the band.

David and I attended the annual Stinger Band concert, directed by Mike Pierce. I sat astounded at the harmony, diversity of musical styles, and the incredible blend of sound from the various instruments. The music delighted the hearer. This is amazing when you consider most of the musicians do not live in Lake City and were only here for practices for perhaps only hours. Yet the instruments brought forth such beautiful music.

Paul likens our bodies to instruments. We can use our physical body, our thoughts, attitudes, and desires for sin or use our body for righteousness to bring glory to God. Paul also tells us "Consider yourselves to be dead to sin, but alive to God in Christ Jesus. (Romans 6:11) The word "consider" in Greek means to calculate by adding up the facts presented in verses 1-10 and then act accordingly.

The new life is based on our union with Christ. All that a person is before salvation is made "old" by reason of the presence of the new life in Christ. (Romans 6:6) As believers and followers of Christ we are separated from the power of the old life. However, the presence of the old life self has not been eradicated.

We have the responsibility to not let sin reign in our body, nor to obey human lusts. In other words, don't use your body as an instrument of sin to unrighteousness. But yield your body as an instrument of righteousness because we are to be alive to God and dead to sin.

Daily, many times over, we make choices to use our body for sin or for righteousness. Which will you do?

This is NOT a Trail

...observe what the LORD your God requires: Walk in his ways, and keep his decrees and commands, his laws and requirements, as written in the Law of Moses, so that you may prosper in all you do and wherever you go. 1 Kings 2:3 (NIV)

"THIS IS NOT A TRAIL" the sign read. We had spent the day topping Red Cloud and then Sunshine. I was beat and so were my hiking partners. We had sat resting when a "runner" came whizzing by taking the "not a trail". I asked him about the path. He answered, "It's doable and shorter than the marked trail."

Usually, I am good about heeding signs. Exhausted, I proceeded to persuade the others to take "not a trail." I succeeded; we began the descent. It did not take long to determine that the "not a trail" was treacherous, steep, covered by large loose rocks, and barely discernible. Unwilling to turn back and admit I had made a mistake we followed "not a trail' till it met THE trail. The shortcut was no shortcut. Because of my "disobedience" we suffered sore feet and muscles, bruises and scrapes from falls (it could have been worse), it took longer and worst of all, my husband reminds me of my bad choice that day.

Just as the warning sign I read that day, God provides warning signs for us. The Lord's commandments lead us to life and not death, blessings and not cursing, victory and not defeat, abundance not insufficiency, purposeful living not dissatisfaction. God's commandments are not to keep us from having fun; they are for our protection and blessing.

God gives us signposts to warn, help, protect, and guide us. Sometime we ignore His Words because we think we know better or we think the rules do not apply to us. That is pride. We think God's way is too hard when in fact the opposite is true.

God's warning signs keep us from sin and help us live for His glory. They also lead us to joy, peace, purpose, satisfaction, abundant life and eternal life.

Have I been looking for God? Am I paying attention? Don't detour from God's path. Check the signs.

One of the many waterfalls on Cataract Gulch Trail

Living in a Foreign Land

But Daniel resolved not to defile himself with the royal food and wine, and he asked the chief official for permission not to defile himself this way.
Daniel 1:8 (NIV)

Once, I was in a British Colony for the Fourth of July. There were no barbecues, red, white and blues, no fireworks. Eerily, British citizens went on with their daily lives with no acknowledgment of what I considered "my sacred heritage celebration."

Daniel was in foreign land, not as a visitor, but as a slave. As a Hebrew captive, he served three pagan regimes. Given a heathen name, he was assigned a daily ration of food from the king's kitchen that was not kosher. Trained for three years, he entered the royal service as a government official and "interpreter of dreams."

Why this indoctrination or re-programming? It was simple, the Babylonians desired to have faithful servants and citizens. By this methodical means the Israelite slaves were to forget their homeland, their heritage, and their God, and become comfortable with their bondage by adopting the heathen practices of their jailers.

Daniel was resolute. He determined not to defile himself. Like Daniel, we are called to live out our faith in an alien environment. Our citizenship is not of this world.

I have given them your word and the world has hated them, for they are not of the world any more than I am of the world. John 17:14 (NIV)

You are a chosen generation, a royal priesthood, an holy nation, a peculiar people; that ye should show forth the praises of him who hath called you out of darkness into his marvelous light." 1 Peter 2:9

For our citizenship is in heaven, from which also we eagerly wait for a Savior, the Lord Jesus Christ. Philippians 3:21

Do not be conformed to this world." Romans 12:1

Like Daniel, "alien" philosophies attempt to suck us under, to make us forget our homeland, that is heaven, our heritage, a chosen people, and our God. If we are to stand against the tide, we must purpose in our heart not to be defiled by the world.

Read the book of Daniel and make a list of traits of Daniel's life. This will give you an understanding of what it means to determine "not to defile yourself."

Polaris

Jesus Christ the same yesterday, today, and for ever. Hebrews 13:8 (KJV)

Ask anyone in Lake City about Polaris and nearly all will say that Polaris is a corporation that produces off road vehicles — snowmobiles and ATV's, and accessories. A military man may tell you that Polaris was a two-stage solid-fuel nuclear armed submarine launched ballistic missile build during the Cold War.

Polaris is also another name for the North Star or Pole Star, part of the Little Dipper, and is easily visible over the skies of Lake City.

Polaris doesn't budge. It sits motionless while the innumerable stars revolve around it. Polaris sits due north no matter where you go in the northern hemisphere. This makes Polaris the single most important celestial point outside of the sun.

Today, with GPS, Polaris may not seem as crucial as it used to be. But you can still use it to know where you are, where you came from, and even where you're going.

More amazing is the constancy of our God. *Jesus Christ is the same yesterday, today, and forever.* There it stands as an absolute proposition that our God does not change. Our Savior is always the same. He is not fickle, inconsistent, erratic, or indecisive. His character and plans are fixed. His decrees, laws, commands and truths stand forever.

These words are an encouragement when everything and everyone and every situation are changing. Our God is immutable — steady, invariable, stable, unwavering, unchallengeable, and unchanging.

But more than an encouragement for our circumstances, this truth should be an encouragement for right living, holiness, commitment, forgiveness, faithfulness and perseverance. Our culture is ever changing and it wants to change us. The truth that God is unchangeable is a source of confidence as we stand and proclaim the good news and oppose what our culture accepts.

Jesus Christ is our Polaris. For many He is not considered crucial to their existence or their future. But like Polaris, He is a constant to know where you are, where you came from, and even where you're going.

Polaris

God's Faithfulness

Yesterday morning, I was sitting in front of the heater, thinking about our shopping excursion the previous day and the ever so slight increase in the price of almost everything. Ink cartridges have gone up more than 16%, gas 28%, and food 13% and that is just since last January.

Mentally I was grumbling and complaining at no one in particular, maybe feeling a little sorry for myself wondering how we are going to pay our propane bill, the doctor bills, and the mountain of other bills.

Then a verse came to mind, *I was young and now I am old, yet I have never seen the righteous forsaken or their children begging bread.* Psalm 37:25 (NIV)

People With Pretty Feet

How beautiful on the mountains are the feet of those who bring good news, who proclaim peace, who bring good tidings, who proclaim salvation, who say to Zion, "Your God reigns!" Isaiah 52:7 (NIV)

God has made many beautiful things but I do not think of feet as being particularly pretty. I would not even rate it in the top ten most beautiful body parts. But to God "feet" are beautiful. Why feet? What is it about feet that God thinks is so beautiful? Why not lips? It takes a mouth to tell others about Christ. Why not hands? Hands provide service.

Feet move us from one place to another. Jesus commanded, *"Go therefore into all the world and preach the gospel to all creation."* (Mark 16:16) God sends messengers, those who will share the good news of the gospel, but for them to "go" they must move and that takes feet.

But having feet does not necessarily mean that one goes. That takes willingness, a desire to go. But even willingness is not enough. One must obey. It takes putting one foot in front of the other and moving. Go. I think that is the clincher, that's what makes ones feet beautiful, an obedient heart.

Take a look at your feet. Beautiful feet and an obedient heart go together.

Good Luck Charms

Saint Patrick is known for driving the "snakes" that is, the devil, from Ireland. The Irish have adopted the shamrock, and in its rare form, the four leaf clover, as a symbol of the "luck of the Irish." This Irish symbolism becomes prevalent in American culture once a year as we celebrate Saint Patrick's Day and also lives on throughout the year in the form of a famous cereal that included moons, stars, hearts and clovers.

The act of carrying a lucky charm, or talisman, has been part of many cultures throughout history. Charms and talismans serve two purposes: first to attract good luck and secondly to ward off evil. A rabbit's foot, a lucky penny, a horseshoe or just something a person perceives as bringing good luck, like the basketball player who wears the same pair of socks when playing opponents or the hunter who carries his "lucky" gun.

A good luck charm, this is what the Israelites perceived the Ark of God as, at least in the account in 1 Samuel 4. Israel had engaged in battle with the Philistines. They were defeated and lost 4000 men on the battlefield. In verse 3, they asked the elders, *"Why has the Lord defeated us today before the Philistines?"* Then they have this "brilliant" idea. *"Let us take to ourselves from Shiloh the ark of the covenant of the Lord, that it may come among us and deliver us from the power of our enemies."*

In their wilderness wanderings, it was above the Ark that the pillar of fire and the cloud were seen. It was when the Ark set out that Moses said, "*Rise up, O Lord! And let your enemies be scattered, and let those who hate you flee before you.*" Numbers 10:35

So why not use the ark to win the battle? Surely we will win if we have God's presence? They thought that by taking the Ark into battle they would be assured victory over the enemy. This was not the case. They are soundly defeated, 30,000 of their warriors are killed and the Ark is captured by the Philistines. How could this happen? Why would God's people suffer such loss and humiliation, especially since they had the Ark?

What the Israelites failed to realize is that the Ark was the symbol of God's presence, not the presence of God, there is an immense difference.

The symbol or the presence, what do we have? We have church, Bible study, Christian TV, Christian Music and many other religious activities. But the bottom line is, "Do we have the presence of God?"

Thanksgiving

For although they knew God, they neither glorified him as God nor gave thanks to him, but their thinking became futile and their foolish hearts were darkened. Romans 1:21 (NIV)

In Lake City, we honor the holiday with vacation from school, a community Thanksgiving service and community dinner. It is time for the Turkey Trot, an event to raise funds for Toys for Tots. Paul writes to people who knew God. He lists the steps to idolatry: they knew God; they did not honor God; they did not give thanks to God; their thinking became futile; their hearts were darkened.

The truth about God demands that we, His creation, glorify Him as the Creator. When we don't, we fail in the purpose for which we were created. It started with Adam and Eve. From Eden to Lake City, people are bent toward disobedience. It is in our spiritual genetic code. There is a problem honoring God and giving thanks to God.

How do we fail to honor God and give thanks? What are the signs and symptoms of an ungrateful heart?

Negativity is complaining about little things, sometimes moodiness. Our minds are not deeply rooted in a positive or thankful pattern of thinking. When something pushes our buttons, we quickly forget the goodness of God and begin to grumble.

We are often bitter or unforgiving. In Matthew 18, an unthankful servant is forgiven a great debt, but could not forgive his servant of a much smaller debt.

Bitterness holds things against others and is the result of an unthankful heart.

There is discontentment and greed. Unthankful people always want more. This shows up subtly in Christians, thinking about things we don't have, rather than things we do have. This is a form of greediness.

Boredom leads to frustration, when we fail to take note of everyday miracles, friends, blessings or just being bored with our surroundings.

There is a lukewarm apathy, a loss of zeal for God. The result is a broken relationship with God, unfaithfulness in church attendance, a lack of concern for others, and no heart for church leaders or missionaries and their work.

Ungratefulness and not giving thanks is a serious sin with dire consequences. Read the results in the remainder of the first chapter of Romans.

What steps must we take, every day, to have a grateful heart and a thankful spirit?

An Acts 1:8 Church

I was asked to give a presentation on "How Doing and Supporting Missions has Changed our Church." This gave me pause to reflect on our 11 years at Lake City First Baptist Church and the alterations that had taken place as a result of an emphasis on the Great Commission. Financial support has significantly increased, members have personally involved themselves in mission trips, and others have gone and stayed in full time ministry. There are two ministries that have been initiated in Lake City. I am certain God has done even more.

Does this make us an Acts 1:8 Church? I went to the Book of Acts to examine characteristics of the newly birthed church. This is what I found.

1:14—They met together and were constantly united in prayer.
2:37-38—God's Word went forth and pierced hearts and there was repentance.
2:42—All the believers devoted themselves to the apostles' teaching and to fellowship and to sharing in meals, including the Lord's Supper, and to prayer.
2:43—A deep sense of awe came overthem all...many miraculous signs and wonders.
2:44-45 —They sold their property and possessions and shared the money with those in need.
2:47—The Lord added to the church daily.
4:33—There was great power to witness of the resurrection of the Lord Jesus and great grace was upon them all.

5:11—There was great fear.

5:12-14—More miraculous signs and wonders among the people and more and more people believed and were brought to the Lord, crowds of both men and women.

6:1-7—Rumblings of discontent led to taking care of the widows, the disenfranchised.

6:8—There were more amazing miracles and signs among the people.

8:1—There was a great persecution against the church.

Acts 1:8 Church? God's word is the measure but it is interesting to note that the command of Acts 1:8, *"....you will be my witnesses, telling people about me everywhere — in Jerusalem, throughout Judea, in Samaria, and to the ends of the earth"* was not carried out until Acts 8:1 when there was great persecution.

My conclusion is we will not have an Acts 1:8 church until we have an Acts 8:1 church.

Memorial Day

Memorial Day is a day of remembrance for those who have died in our nation's service. Memorial Day was officially proclaimed on May 5, 1868, by General John Logan, in his General Order No. 11, and was first observed on May 30, 1868, when flowers were placed on the graves of Union and Confederate soldiers at Arlington National Cemetery.

As a child, I remember the men who stood on the street corner selling "poppies" and asking "Why?" My mother explained, but I must admit it went over my childish brain. Many years have passed and the traditional observance of Memorial Day has diminished. Many Americans nowadays have forgotten the meaning and traditions of Memorial Day. At many cemeteries, the graves of the fallen are increasingly ignored, neglected.

On a recent vacation, we stopped for breakfast at a café in St. Anthony, Idaho. Startling were the hundreds of pictures of men and women of St. Anthony who died serving these United States, from the Civil War to present military conflicts. It was sobering to slowly gaze and read of the many who sacrificed their lives for my liberty. I cried in shame and humility. Later that day, as we passed several cemeteries, I noted Americans flags flying proudly over scores of graves and again tears flowed down my cheek.

But as I pondered Memorial Day, a scripture invaded my thoughts. *Therefore, since we are surrounded by such a great cloud of witnesses, let us throw off everything that hinders and the sin that so easily entangles, and let us run with perseverance the race marked out for us. Let us fix our eyes on Jesus, the author and perfecter of our faith, who for the joy set before him endured the cross, scorning its shame, and sat down at the right hand of the throne of God.* Hebrews 12:1-2 (NIV)

Like the portraits in the café and the flags in the cemeteries that remind me of sacrificial lives, I am to understand and appreciate that there are heroes of the Faith who have fought and sacrificed to see that I have the opportunity to hear and accept the freedom that one can have in Christ. Unlike those American patriots that are buried and gone, ours "Faith veterans" are crowded together, watching and cheering me forward. How can we follow in their footsteps? It is by laying aside the sins and faults that hinder and running with endurance the race God has set before each of us.

Like the heroes that we recognize on Memorial Day, who have left us a legacy of democracy and patriotism, I too want to leave a legacy, a legacy of faith. May it be said of me, "She was Faithful."

"Be kind whenever possible. It is always possible."
Tenzin Gyatso, 14th Dalai Lama

Leave No Trace

Whoever can be trusted with very little can also be trusted with much, and whoever is dishonest with very little will also be dishonest with much.
Luke 16:10 (NIV)

Posted along many Hinsdale County Trails is a phrase, "LEAVE NO TRACE." Leave no trace is a plan that encourages people to be more concerned about their environment and to protect it for future generations. The idea is to leave the places you enjoy, as good or better, than you found them. This is accomplished though small, simple decisions: staying on trails, manage your pet, leave what you find, respect other visitors, and take your trash. These small actions take care of our recreational resources that we cherish and everyone benefits.

Often we underestimate the importance of our small actions. Not stopping for a stop sign, when there is no traffic and no one will see, or keeping the incorrect change in our favor given mistakenly by the cashier, or not returning phone calls, or throwing trash out along the trail. But the words of Christ point to the significance of small actions and our faithfulness to obey or be kind in what might seem trivial or inconsequential.

How we act or respond when no one is observing is who we are. It is an expression of our true character and where our love and devotion truly lie. Faithfulness in small choices of behavior reveals what's in the heart.

Are the fruits of your spirit honesty, gentleness, patience, and loving kindness? Is your life conforming to the image of Christ? Do "minor" actions display the love of Christ and bring glory to God?

It is in the small disciplines of life that Christ like character is formed. Only by faithfulness in little things are we trained to act righteously when we are under pressure.

Often we equate noble and great deeds with worth. We look to perform important tasks and accomplishments. Today live life being faithful in little things.

"I long to accomplish a great and noble task, but it is my chief duty to accomplish small tasks as if they were great and noble." — Helen Keller

"Be faithful in small things because it is in them that your strength lies." — Mother Teresa

Faithful

Devoted, committed, dependable ~ living deliberately in observing our grown son and daughter's behavior with each other and with their aged grandparents, is to see the teachings of their childhood come full circle. *Train up a child in the way he should go: and when he is old, he will not depart from it.*
Proverbs 22:6

Living with purpose and thoughtfulness, living with the prayer 'to whom much is given, much is expected' was the mantra with which our son and daughter grew up.

Their dad and I spent our money more on such events and investments as education, concerts, theater, travel and books rather than the biggest house, newest cars or designer clothes affordable.

Though our grown son and daughter have demanding work and full lives and do not live nearby their grandparents, the younger folks have consistently let the aged folks know that they love and honor their grandparents with regular phone calls and video chats via the internet, frequently sending Ensure and other non-perishable healthy snacks and flying across the country and even from out of the country to be with their grandma and grandpa.

Just as when her brother, and sister-in-law, graduated from Notre Dame with their PhD's in aerospace engineering, our daughter, like her parents and grandparents, was proud and would not have missed the official celebrations for anything, and so it was when his sister graduated from Brandeis University with a masters in sustainable international development. Our son brought his wife and baby son across the country for us all to be together for the official celebrations.

It was fitting that while in the area we went to Walden Pond, where Thoreau said, "I went to the woods because I wished to live deliberately, to front only the essential facts of life, and see if I could not learn what it had to teach, and not, when I came to die, discover that I had not lived. I did not wish to live what was not life, living is so dear; nor did I wish to practice resignation, unless it was quite necessary. I wanted to live deep and suck out all the marrow of life."

Gentleness

It was unexpected gentleness. A glorious day in May and I was sitting by the river with my Sheltie dog, Spring, when we suddenly heard baby bird noises and up from the water's edge waddled this tiny yellow creature! Though Spring and the duckling had never seen a living thing like each other before they knew instinctively that trustworthy friends don't have to be exactly alike!

I think that God shall never send a gift so precious as a trustworthy friend!

Gentle Pleasures

The tangerine colored morning sky made me smile as I grabbed my camera ~ what an exquisite way to start the day!

The heavens declare the glory of God; the skies proclaim the work of his hands. Psalm 19:1 (NIV)

My husband's morning call from the office makes me happy! Thinking about us brings an abundance of good memories sprinkled with love, laughter and playfulness!

Our dogs, Spring and Joy, make me laugh!

The cozy crackling fire and the promise of this new day is inspiring!

How can people live bored, uninterested in daily life...to waste such a precious gift; do something, make changes! Appreciate your blessings!

To again quote Robert Louis Stevenson: "The world is so full of a number of things, I'm sure we should all be as happy as kings."

And Mother Teresa: "Once you choose hope, everything is possible."

Cairns

Hiking the many trails around Lake City, often you see a stack of stones. It is man-made where hikers have left a mark that they had passed that way or perhaps, a marker for direction. When I first began hiking the area, I thought it was fun to make my contribution to the effort and carefully add my stone, balancing it atop the monument. Later I learned that these are Cairns.

Cairns are reminders that someone was here before. Someone else has walked this path, passed this way, stopped in this place, and took the time to make a contribution. A cairn is a tangible reminder of the past.

In Joshua 4 God gave Joshua a command to build two Cairns: Joshua called out the twelve men whom he selected from the People of Israel, one man from each tribe.

Joshua directed them, "Cross to the middle of the Jordan and take your place in front of the Chest of God, your God. Each of you heft a stone to your shoulder, a stone for each of the tribes of the People of Israel, so you'll have something later to mark the occasion. When your children ask you, 'What are these stones to you?' you'll say, 'The flow of the Jordan was stopped in front of the Chest of the Covenant of God as it crossed the Jordan—stopped in its tracks. These stones are a permanent memorial for the People of Israel." Joshua 4:6-7 (The Message)

The stone memorials were to point future generations to a God of miracles and might. A God who faithfully guides, protects, and works on behalf of His people. He is a God who is deserving of honor, reverence, and trust. In times of doubt and difficulty it would be a reminder of what God did for them.

At times, we need to remember and remind ourselves of the Holy God, His majesty, His power, His Person, and yes, even His love and care of us. How do you strengthen your faith and those of others with reminders of who God is and what He has done?

First Baptist Church — Lake City

Powderhorn Lakes Trail

But God, who is rich in mercy, for his great love wherewith he loved us, Even when we were dead in sins, hath quickened us together with Christ, (by grace ye are saved;) And hath raised us up together, and made us sit together in heavenly places in Christ Jesus: Ephesians 2:4-6

At the end of Indian Creek Road is the Powderhorn Lakes trailhead. The trail climbs through a Spruce forest, a large meadow and goes back into the woods. After a steep climb it emerges in a meadow beside some beaver ponds. Here, the trail splits. Follow the right fork to the lower lake. The trail skirts the west side of the lower lake and follows the creek to the upper lake. The lakes themselves are set in a beautiful basin.

Uncle Jerry and I hiked this trail. What an adventure. The hike was a spur of the moment decision. Leaving our group, we started the ascent with water, food, and rain gear and a determination to see the lakes. Reaching the lower lake we sat and enjoyed our lunch and then continued to the upper lake.

Moments later we found shelter under some spruce while we waited out an afternoon hail storm that turned into a downpour. On the return trip much of the trail was a flowing stream. The trek continued for six hours. We often had to stop and rest. Sitting on a log, resting in drizzling rain, Uncle Jerry quoted, *"God has raised us up together, and made us sit together in heavenly places in Christ Jesus."*

We think of "in heavenly places" as just that, in heaven. However, this phrase, only found four times, designates the heavenly places as any place where the lordship of Christ is in operation.

Heavenly places are not some sector of celestial geography. They are the centers at and from which Christ is already running His new creation. So Christians right now are "sitting with Him in the heavenly places" whether curled up in a chair at home, sitting behind the wheel, in a wheelchair, in a dentist's chair, or not sitting anywhere in particular.

The accent is not on the posture or position, but on the quality of life. "Heavenly" designates a life where Christ is Lord and Master and all that is important is Him. We reside in heavenly places when we are living His will and not our own.

Are you living in heavenly places? If not, now is the time to let Christ rule in your life.

Sleepless Part 1

Search me O God and know my heart; try me, and know my thoughts: And see if there be any wicked way in me, and lead me in the way everlasting. Psalm 139:23-24

I did not sleep well last night. When I don't get enough sleep, I am grouchy, ache all over and I am just generally unpleasant. But today, I determined I was not going to be that way. I resolved that no one would even know that I didn't sleep.

THEN my husband happened. "You didn't sleep last night. It's in your attitude."

This hit me like a ton of bricks. Now I was angry. I sat though our devotion time fuming. "Who is *he* to talk about *my* attitude?"

Then I thought about the Beatitudes and my desire to have these attitudes.

Perhaps, like me, today you need to pray, "*Search me O God and know my heart; try me, and know my thoughts: And see if there be any wicked way in me, and lead me in the way everlasting.*"

Each of us needs to examine ourselves, letting God search our hearts.

Sleepless
Part 2

I lie awake thinking of you, meditating on you through the night. Psalm 63:6

I stay awake through the night, thinking about your promise. Psalm 119:148

These words were penned by David, who is known as a man after the heart of God.

I have often thought that David had insomnia, for frequently he mentions sleep.

But these verses would refute my perception. He writes, "I lie awake thinking" and "I stay awake through the night." This gives the impression that David intended to spend this time in prayer.

Personally, I love to sleep, even more so now than when I was a teen. I guess it is because I am not a good sleeper. It is frustrating when I cannot sleep. I cannot say, like David, that I intentionally stay awake to meditate on God or to think about His promise.

However, when I do find myself tossing and turning, sleeplessness is not wasted time, if I do like David—recounting His blessings, praising His intervention in my life, worshiping His majesty, glorifying His name. When I do this, instead of being lost to idle time, these occasions become treasured moments alone with God.

A Day in God's Courts

"A Day in the mountains is better than a month in the city." I know this is true, because I grew up in the city and frequently return there to visit my mom and our daughters. It is a take on the John Muir quote, "One day's exposure to mountains is better than cartloads of books." I love books. I love to read, but to experience the mountains is to breathe in calmness, strength, and an awareness of the creator that I fail to miss amid the activity of a metropolis.

However, David in the Psalms tells of where he would rather spend a day, "A single day in your courts is better than a thousand anywhere else!" "I long, yes, I faint with longing to enter the courts of the Lord with my whole being, body and soul, I will shout joyfully to the living God."

Why does the Psalmist cherish God's house?   Look again at Psalm 84.

He understands that his house is where God dwells. "*How lovely is your dwelling place, O Lord of Heaven's armies.*" He knew he could be in the presence of God there and meet with God.

It is a place of joy. "*What joy for those who can live in your house, always singing praises.*"   David knew a lot about stress and adversity. He knew about the guilt and despair. In God's house, in God's presence he could find a place of repentance, acceptance and experience the joy that only God provides.

The goodness of God is experienced in His presence, in His house.

"For the Lord God is our sun and our shield. He gives us grace and glory. The Lord will withhold no good thing from those who do what is right." Psalms 84:11

Everyone occasionally is absent from Sunday worship, but there is a laxness in weekly worship attendance. It is as if we consider church attendance as optional.

The writers of Hebrews is explicit, *Let us not give up meeting together, as some are in the habit of doing, but let us encourage one another — and all the more as you see the Day approaching.*
Hebrews 10:25 (NIV)

The Wisdom of the Wilderness

We need the wisdom of the wilderness just as Moses did, Jesus did and Paul did, as the wilderness is the open, unencumbered place to find God. What grace we are given living here in God's Cathedral of Lake City to have such access to so many holy places as Moses, Jesus and Paul did.

But ask the animals, and they will teach you,
or the birds in the sky, and they will tell you;
or speak to the earth, and it will teach you,
or let the fish in the sea inform you.
Which of all these does not know that
the hand of the LORD has done this?
In his hand is the life of every creature and
the breath of all mankind. Job 12:7-10 (NIV)

Lake San Cristobal

Praise the LORD.

Praise the LORD from the heavens;
praise him in the heights above.
Praise him, all his angels; praise
him, all his heavenly hosts.
Praise him, sun and moon;
praise him, all you shining stars.
Praise him, you highest heavens
and you waters above the skies.
Let them praise the name of the LORD, for
at his command they were created,
and he established them for ever and ever—
he issued a decree that will never pass away.
Praise the LORD from the earth,
you great sea creatures and all ocean depths,
lightning and hail, snow and clouds,
stormy winds that do his bidding,
you mountains and all hills,
fruit trees and all cedars,
wild animals and all cattle,
small creatures and flying birds,
kings of the earth and all nations,
you princes and all rulers on earth,
young men and maidens, old men and children.
Let them praise the name of the LORD,
for his name alone is exalted;
his splendor is above the earth and the heavens.
He has raised up for his people a horn,
the praise of all his saints, of Israel,
the people close to his heart.
Praise the LORD.

Psalm 148 (NIV)

Providence

Listening to the dramatized biographies of John Newton and William Wilberforce I was struck by one reoccurring word that each used in recounting the events of their lives — providence.

Providence is the foreseeing care and guidance of God or nature over the creatures of the earth; God, especially when conceived as omnisciently directing the universe and the affairs of humankind with wise benevolence; a manifestation of divine care or direction.

"God's providence in history" was a common term in the early 1400's and frequently used by our founding fathers. The pilgrims in 1621 "resolved to be thankful for God's providence — which included the gifts of life and friendship." Roger Williams, after being banished from Massachusetts trudged through the snow for 14 weeks. Where he settled, he named the new town Providence, attributing it to God's care and direction. Benjamin Franklin, though many consider him to have been a man of questionable faith in God, spoke frequently of his belief that God Himself was directing the parties who led the Revolution. Using the colonial term "Providence," Franklin penned "The longer I live, the more convincing proofs I see of this truth, that God governs in the affairs of men. And if a sparrow cannot fall to the ground without His notice, is it probable that an empire can rise without His aid?"

Bible authors did not use the word providence, but its meaning was recognized as "the hand of the Lord."

Ezra recounted, "The king gave him everything he asked for because the gracious hand of the Lord his God was on him." As the children of Israelites left Egypt, the Egyptians recognized the "hand of God." In Judges, "the hand of the Lord was against them for evil because of their sin.

Providence, though an outdated word is still evident in the affairs of men and nations. Often we do not attribute to God the events of our country or our own lives, but as a child of God, He is directing our steps. He leads and guides and gives us favor.

Good and bad occurrences are in the providence of God. Consider yourself and 99% of the population of Lake City, in the providence of God, you have been led here. We may think it "just" happened or we "decided" to move here.

In his heart a man plans his course, but the LORD determines his steps. Proverbs 16:9 (NIV)

Make no mistake. You are here, in this place, by God's providence. And who knows, but that you came here for just such a time in history.

Church

My temple will be called a house of prayer for all nations,' but you have turned it into a den of thieves.
Mark 11:17 and Isaiah 56:7 and Jeremiah 7:11

In front of St. James Episcopal Church here in Lake City there hangs a small sign with an invitation, "Open for Prayer." 24/7 this church proclaims the message of this scripture. The other churches are also open for prayer, but St. James alone announces to the world this is a "house of prayer." Anyone can meet God here, any time of the day or night; God is standing by, geared up to meet with them.

God calls his dwelling place "a house of prayer." You and I are the "temple" in which God also lives. Don't you realize that all of you together are the temple of God and that the Spirit of God lives in you?"
1 Corinthians 3:16

So, if God calls his dwelling place "a house of prayer" and God lives in us, are we as individuals also to be a 'house of prayer'?

Can people recognize us as a "house of prayer"?

Pastor Ed Nettleton often has summarized the teachings of Paul by stating "You are the body of Christ, now act like it."

Self Control

My Stuff.

Recently I wanted to buy a women's magazine. As I viewed the menagerie of newsstand offerings I noted the common topics — the latest diets, scrumptious recipes, "look younger, be healthier", etc.; all longtime subjects that women are interested in. But this time I observed a new reoccurring theme, "Clutter" and "Get Organized." I always see these articles around the New Years, but now it seems that every periodical has an article about reducing clutter, the things that we accumulate. The dictionary defines clutter as a collection of things lying about an untidy mess; when there is so much stuff that you can't make any sense out of it.

Stuff — why do we have it, want it, and have such a hard time parting with it?

We define ourselves by our stuff — great wardrobe, beautiful jewelry, latest electronic gadget, how many tools we own, newest model vehicle, etc. We seem to think we are our stuff — it's bombarding us all day on TV, online, billboards, and in a hundred other ways. Even as Christians we get caught up in the cycle of buying new things to replace the things we already own.

We think things can make us happy and satisfied. People often buy things because they are trying to fill a void within them — emotionally or spiritually. I remember telling someone I was depressed so I was going to buy a new dress. Buying more is an attempt to fill the need for something more. We buy to feel loved, to feel secure, and to feel valued.

We attach our lives and worth to our things. Like defining ourselves by our things, we often define our worth by them as well. How often have you thought highly of someone because of something they owned? We equate human value to item value. We also keep things for the memories they bring even though we can have the memories without the things.

Clutter is a problem for anyone, but for Christians, it spells major trouble. Clutter does more than affect us physically and emotionally; it affects us spiritually because it keeps us from following Jesus fully. We simply cannot make room for Him when so many other things are in the way. The more we stay focused on the junk of this life, the less time and energy we have to focus on the important matters: God and His plans for our lives.

Christ said, *Lay not up for yourselves treasures upon earth, where moth and rust doth corrupt, and where thieves break through and steal: But lay up for yourselves treasures in heaven, where neither moth nor rust doth corrupt, and where thieves do not break through nor steal: For where your treasure is, there will your heart be also.* Matthew 6:19-21

Teach Us to Number Our Days

I am ashamed to say that sometimes I waste time. I don't know why I can't remember that I am always working for God. He has given me this gift and I have to answer to him for how I used it.

I have seen numerous people on the threshold of death and for that moment they mellow, but when they recover, they mostly grow back into their old ways and seem to think that they again have unlimited time. They have learned little or nothing about positive change.

"Time is what we want most, but what we use worst." William Penn

"Those who make the worse use of their time are the first to complain of its shortness." Jean DeLa Bruyere

"In truth, people can generally make time for what they choose to do; it is not really the time but the will that is lacking." Sir John Lubbock

So teach us to number our days, that we may apply our hearts unto wisdom. Psalm 90:12 (KJV)

Self esteem

Walking the dogs along the Henson Creek path, toward the ice climbing rocks, I stopped to watch the climbers. There were people in wheel chairs, people with a leg missing. Some climbers had no legs. It was like watching an inspirational documentary.

"When we do the best we can, we never know what miracle is wrought in our life, or in the life of another." — Helen Keller

For the Unemployed

"Heavenly Father, we remember before you those who suffer want and anxiety from lack of work. Guide the people of this land so to use our public and private wealth that all may find suitable and fulfilling employment, and receive just payment for their labor; through Jesus Christ our Lord. Amen." (BCP)

A Peak Experience

About eight days after Jesus said this, he took Peter, John and James with him and went up onto a mountain to pray. As he was praying, the appearance of his face changed, and his clothes became as bright as a flash of lightning. Two men, Moses and Elijah, appeared in glorious splendor, talking with Jesus. They spoke about his departure, which he was about to bring to fulfillment at Jerusalem.
Luke 9:28-31(NIV)

There are more mountains in Hinsdale County than I could climb in my lifetime. However, I have topped my share, including the five fourteeners. Each peak is a challenge that takes resilience, strength, and determination to reach the summit. It is exhilarating to stand atop a mountain, lift my arms in a "Rocky" pose, turn 360° and marvel at God's creation; to praise Him for this unbelievable opportunity and privilege to be standing there and that I had the stamina to make it. It is truly a "peak" experience.

Christians use the term "mountain top" experience; a place of personal closeness to God when He makes His presence and glory known, a powerful encounter that is life changing. This is what happened that day on the Mount of Transfiguration. Luke loves to mention that Jesus prayed. He adds references to prayer at numerous points in the stories he shares with Matthew and Mark; for example in verses 18, 28, 29. It was out of Jesus' normal practice of prayer that this visionary experience arose.

In his sleepiness Peter wants to keep the experience—to pin it down, make it permanent. "*Let's build shrines *for each of you; so that you and we can stay here together."* How can we possibly go back to ordinary life after this? But Moses and Elijah know better. They appeared in glory, says Luke, but were talking with Jesus about how he was going to die in Jerusalem and fulfill God's plan in doing so — his *inglorious* future, the rejection, torture, and death. Then a new glory that comes with the resurrection and our future glory with Him. But this is dependent on the journey Jesus will now take, down the mountain to the suffering, dishonor and death. The disciples recoil with horror when Jesus announced it to them (22). But that's it. The way to heaven is not via the mountaintop, but through the valley, where the cross awaits. True, glorious, mountaintop experiences are like Elijah's night under the broom tree (1 King 19:4-8), giving strength for the long journey a head.

How have your mountaintop experiences given you strength? Thank God for them and pray for sufficient strength for today.

On Playing God

Have you ever wished you were God? If I were God I would have world peace. If I were God everyone would have a place to live, food to eat, clothes to wear. If I were God I would strike this or that person with lightening. If I were God I would...

Everyone has acted as if we are God — doing own thing, not consulting Him before a decision, we pray, "Do this God or do that God. "We all have what I call, "A God Complex."

If you are a parent you have been god to your children. As babies they were totally dependent upon you, to provide love and affection, food and clothing, warmth and shelter. As they grew you found joy in teaching them and taking pride in their accomplishments. But as they grew, they also became independent and you lost some of your status as "god."

Recently I have been playing god. You see, I have a new puppy, Kate. Kate is teaching me a lot about what God has to put up with. I love Kate and I want her to be happy and obedient. An obedient dog is a happy dog because everybody is happier if Mama is happy.

Housetraining is important to me. The other day she peed in the floor. The moment I spotted the spot I yelled her name. Kate ran to her kennel; she knew she had done something wrong. Yes, I was upset, but I didn't beat her, instead I keep up the training, trying to teach her that going outside is for more than just playing in the snow.

God too gets upset with us, but He doesn't beat us up when we mess up, He just keeps on working with us till we learn the lesson and then He moves on to the next one.

I am trying to teach Kate how to walk with a leash. The leash is for her protection here in town. She pulls against it and crosses in front of me. I rein her back to the left. Isn't this like God? The limits He sets are for our protection, yet we pull and strain against His leading (the rules) when He only wants the best for us.

Kate begs for people food, she wants it. We don't feed Kate our food, it is not good for her and we want her to be healthy. God feeds us with His Holy Word, but sometimes we are like Kate and we want what this culture offers instead of God's Word and teaching. Kate will find a piece of dirty bone on the road and chew on it, Yuk. We do the same thing and God says "yuk, what are they thinking? Don't they know how that filth will hurt them?" God warns us, but we ignore Him, we want what WE want.

Being a dog owner is hard. As her god I work with her every day. God too works with us every day — I get tired of the same lessons. I wonder if God gets tired of us making the same mistakes. Regardless, I love little Kate and I will keep working with her — just like God is working on me!

My Dog Kate

"Kate is driving me crazy!" These are the words of my husband.

Kate is our 2 year old Blue Heeler. She is a fabulous dog. She is smart and obeys, for the most part. She is potty trained, good with kids and social with other dogs. So why does she get on my husband's nerves?

It's the ball. Kate loves for you to throw the ball. She chases it, brings it back and waits expectantly for you to throw again. When you take her walking she grabs her ball to go. If she doesn't see a ball, she will go look for one before she leaves for a walk. If she can't find a ball, she will find a stick for you to throw for her. She sleeps with her ball on her pillow. Often I see her with her head draping across it. First thing in the morning she will pick her ball up and plop it in front of you hoping you will take a hint and play with her. Through the day while I am working she will come bring me her ball in hopes that I will play with her.

But it isn't just the ball. She wants to be where you are, always close by. She will sit right under your feet. If you are sitting in a chair or on the sofa she will try to put her head in your lap. She will lick your fingers while you are sleeping, should you put them over the side of the bed.

I wish God could say to me, "Candy is driving me crazy!" All she wants to do is spend time with me. She goes to sleep with me on her mind. She wakes up and the first thing she wants to do is be with me. She won't leave home without me and if she can't find me, she will go looking for me. She takes me wherever she goes. She gives me absolutely no peace. She is right here at my footstool.

Of course God would never say that about me or you.

But what if we were like Kate?

"The purpose of life is not to be happy. It is to be useful, to be honorable, to be compassionate, to have it make some difference that you have lived and lived well." Ralph Waldo Emerson

Little Surprises

Returning from town, pulling into the garage, I was about to close the door when I saw a beautiful buck a foot from me!

My husband and I had a winter picnic and hiked up to a frozen waterfall! Dressed in layers with the sunshine and our famous sapphire sky we enjoy many winter hikes. Though this particular winter hike turned from dazzling to abysmal as we climbed; we flinched as the icy winds picked up under the now colorless sky. Yet, the gift of capturing this frozen waterfall on my camera made all unpleasantness more than worthwhile for me!

Even in the bitter winter cold, living in the mountains of Lake City, there are always gentle delights, if we are open to them. That's how it is with God's Love; if we are open to Him. In the midst of sadness, confusion and pain I have been comforted by a kind word, or by caring arms. I smile at my dog's unconditional love. The warm sunshine in winter is soothing. God's reassurance gives me hope. When all else fails, I know the Creator of the universe is infinitely wiser. In part it is the little surprises that make life worth living.

I absolutely think the idea this world accidentally smashed in space, and it all just happened to work out perfectly, is fiction. Therefore, there must be a Creator, and it follows the Creator of the universe loves his creatures.

And God said, "Let the earth bring forth living creatures of every kind: cattle and creeping things and wild animals of the earth of every kind" and it was so. And God made the wild animals of the earth of every kind, and the cattle of every kind, and everything that creeps upon the ground of every kind. And God saw that it was good. Genesis 1:24-25 (KJV)

Truly, there is so very much I do not understand about life, but I know the Creator of the universe is a lot smarter than I am. I am filled with awe living in these mountains. I humbly thank God for these blessings and ask Him to help me keep moving forward in my life. I think we are going to have to stand before our Creator and I pray to be able to say, "Yes Sir, I really did try to do my best." So God, please help me to keep moving forward in all aspects of my life.

Garage Sale

A summer event takes place in July when many community members have garage sales. Whether they are decluttering or just trying to turn "junk" into cash, there are treasures to be bought and sold. Every year, I find something I can't live without. I take pride in my finds and boast of my skills and finesse in bargaining.

One year, during this event, I went to the home of a teacher. She had many things she had once used in her classroom. I bought a variety of notebooks, binders, and other useful supplies. I also bought a poster. The poster looks like a highway sign and simply reads, "No Excuses." Many years later the sign remains hanging in my office. It reminds me I will not have an excuse for not getting my work done, for not paying the bills, for not writing another church bulletin or whatever it is that I try to give an excuse.

An excuse is "an explanation offered to justify or obtain forgiveness." Synonyms provide an explanation: rationalize, cop out, cover up, disguise, and subterfuge. It's what we do when we do not want to own up to our actions. Excuses often come in the form of blaming someone or something or to get out of doing what is required of us. Excuses are prevalent in our culture and to all humanity. No big deal. This is the way we live.

However, God has something to say about making excuses to Him: IT WON'T WORK!

Don't *excuse* yourself by saying, "Look, we didn't know," for God understands all hearts, and He sees you. *If you say, "But we knew nothing about this," does not he who weighs the heart perceive it? Does not he who guards your life know it? Will he not repay each person according to what he has done?* Proverbs 24:12 (NIV)

If I had not come and spoken to them, they would not be guilty of sin. Now, however, they have no excuse for their sin. John 15:22 (NIV)

For since the creation of the world God's invisible qualities — his eternal power and divine nature — have been clearly seen, being understood from what has been made, so that men are without excuse. Romans 1:20 (NIV)

For you are free, yet you are God's slaves, so don't use your freedom as an excuse to do evil. 1 Peter 2:16

No Excuses! What are you making excuses for? What are you excusing in others? How do these need to change?

Using Time Wisely

Wait on the LORD: be of good courage, and he shall strengthen thine heart: wait, I say, on the LORD.
Psalm 27:14 (KJV)

This reminds me of 'Be still and know I am God' Humm...this must be important! Wait! Be still! When I am sitting still looking out on the mountains I am aware of God's presence in a way like no other. There is no telephone, no computer I am not even walking so there is nothing else to do or think about but the presence and peace of God.

I AM thy shield, thy protector. I AM the Lord that heals thee. I AM the comforter. I am the light of the world. I AM the bread of life. I AM the good shepherd. I AM the Way, the Truth and the Life.

Back at work at the computer, a friend emails about how the day has slipped away as they play on the computer. I haven't completed anything yet...too busy on the damn computer...been here all morning. Another email: It is now almost 7:30 and been on this machine for two hours. Have to get off and have some supper.

Like consistently incorporating healthy changes into our lives it takes practice and patience to take time away from all the time sinks: time away from television, time away from computer games or social media and silly emails, time away from shopping, time away from our hobbies and toys, even time away from our work, take the time in your quiet place to be still in the presence of God and he will strengthen our heart.

No Worries

Do not worry about tomorrow, for tomorrow will worry about its own things. Sufficient for the day is its own trouble. Matthew 6:34

Do not be anxious about anything, but in everything, by prayer and petition, with thanksgiving, present your requests to God. Philippians 4:6 (NIV)

I know it is much easier to say, 'Don't worry! Be happy!' To actually do it, is very hard. Does worrying help or solve anything? No, of course not. Often we use up our precious time and energy with needless worry, and the problem or situation remains.

First we must count our blessings, because if we don't, we might as well not even have them. To take one's mind off the worrisome situations, try getting outside. In the healing nature and exercise with gardening or walking, and while doing this somewhat mindless task, fill your mind with peaceful and hopeful thoughts and prayers of thanksgiving.

Observe and learn from mistakes! I have heard it said: it may be an unwise man that doesn't learn from his own mistakes but it is an absolutely foolish person who doesn't learn from other people's mistakes.

Finally, brothers, whatever is true, whatever is noble, whatever is right, whatever is pure, whatever is lovely, whatever is admirable — if anything is excellent or praiseworthy — think about such things.
Philippians 4:8 (NIV)

Hidden Dangers

Guard your heart above all else, for it determines the course of your life. Proverbs 4:23

A blanket of fresh fallen snow covered the street. I left Mocha Moose, my favorite business hangout and source of local information and a place to visit with friends. I carried my latte as I stepped; watching for ice, when "whoops." My feet flew out from under me. Ouch! Falling on ice hurts. Ice is rock hard, incredibly solid, and unforgiving.

Thankfully all that was damaged was my pride; a bruise or two that will soon fade. Others who have taken the same spill and their life was changed forever, broken bones, a concussion, or irreparable head trauma. I was not being reckless or careless, I was on guard. I never saw the danger. I suspected it, but it took me by surprise.

We are warned to guard our hearts above all else. The Hebrew "guard" suggests a blockade, a sentry. The ESV says, "*Keep your heart with all vigilance.*" This means to be keenly watchful to detect danger; ever awake and alert; sleeplessly watchful.

We encounter dangers that attempt to distract us from our Savior. Some are overt, we instantly recognize as a snare of the devil — adultery, lying, pornography, stealing, etc. We also encounter "hidden" dangers, things we do not readily spot — careers, community involvement, recreation, etc.

These are the "cares of this life" that can cause our faith and life in Christ to be stunted and unfruitful. Often we participate in a harmless activity, computer games, watching TV, reading, sports, etc. and before we realize it we are addicted, spending more time on these activities than pursuit of a relationship with Christ.

How do we guard ourselves from these hidden dangers when we are bombarded by a hostile culture and are so easily distracted? The Basics: Develop a relationship with Christ developed through time spent with Him, prayer, Bible reading and study, and church. Make and take opportunity to share Christ with others. Demonstrate who and what we believe with the love of Christ. These are the basics that keep us alert and on guard 24/7, helping us to recognize and protect ourselves from hidden danger.

How are you doing with the basics? Keep a daily log or journal of your efforts.

The Cabin at Waterdog Lake

Iron Men and Women

Therefore, since we are surrounded by such a great cloud of witnesses, let us throw off everything that hinders and the sin that so easily entangles, and let us run with perseverance the race marked out for us. Let us fix our eyes on Jesus, the author and perfecter of our faith. Hebrews 12:1-2a

The San Juan Solstice 50 mile endurance run is a scenic, very difficult loop through the San Juan's. It is for experienced runners only, ultra runners. The run consists of the climb up Alpine Gulch, down William's Creek, a climb to Carson, a long section along the Continental Divide, a descent to Slumgullion Pass, and a final hump up and over the Vicker's Ranch plateau. Altitudes range from 8,600 to 12,800. Terrain and weather conditions change yearly; cold, snowy, windy, dry, muddy or rainy. It takes most runners 10 to 16 hours to finish the course. It is amazing to me there are 200 available spots for runners and the registration limit is filled within a matter of hours.

How do runners prepare themselves? What does it require to finish this grueling race? Months or even years of hard work, early mornings, exercise, obtaining the right equipment, diet and perhaps having a trainer. Consistent and well planned preparation— exercise, diet, even studying the course, the right running shoes, clothes, and of course having nothing to weigh the runner down. There are aid stations where runners are provided water, first aid, nourishment, and needed information and encouragement. But most importantly to finish there must be perseverance. The runner must keep a constant eye on the finish line.

Our walk or run with Christ is compared to a race. The writer of Hebrews admonishes us to strip off every weight that slows us down. Weights are the cares of life, misplaced priorities and values. Our sins can also trip us up and make us stumble. Endurance is vital. Keeping our eyes on Jesus is imperative. In 1 Corinthians 9:24 Paul asks, *"Do you know that in a race all the runners run, but only one gets the prize?"* Then he tells us how to run, *"Run in such a way as to get the prize."*

Like participation in the San Juan Solstice, Christianity is not for sissies. It takes preparation, guidance, commitment, and determination. But as followers of Christ, we have a Champion who is always with us, to give us what we need to win the prize.

River inlet to Lake San Cristobal

Hope for the Future

For I know the plans I have for you," says the LORD. They are plans for good and not for disaster, to give you a future and a hope. Jeremiah 29:11

I think God must give big sighs when I am yet again too concerned about all the details going on with my life so that I get sidetracked.

God sighing...Hello my child, look where you are and what's going on with you...who carried you though all the bad stuff?!

Well...yeah I know...BUT God really...what about this and that and this yet again...still!

Really BIG sigh from God...really...again...my child I love you...I won't let you down...I am here always. Why are you always so surprised?

No kidding God! You are amazing! Where you have brought me is totally miraculous, totally a God-thing! What am I thinking...as YOUR Presence fills the room in the blue of the dawn I bask in the warm fire's glow and see you as I look out on Crystal Peak and feel the PEACE OF GOD...it's just when I say bye God see ya later that I...oh...ah...maybe not so much saying bye for now...

God laughing...thank you!

OK, I'll try...harder...

That's all I ask.

Pray Without Ceasing

"pray without ceasing" 1 Thessalonians 5:17

That is pretty darn clear! The personal way I break that down as not to be overwhelmed with 'PRAYING TO GOD' is to think about my relationships. I love hearing from my grown kids! I love knowing that they are thinking of me and want to talk with me! I love hearing that something I did pleased them! I love hearing about their accomplishments and I appreciate when they share their worries and sadness and talk things over with me.

The same can be said about my spouse and a few trusted friends. You know you are close to someone when you share not only joys, back and forth, but sadness and concerns as well.

God desires a close personal relationship with us. He made us! He loves us! God loves hearing from us! God loves knowing that we are thinking of Him and want to talk with Him! God loves hearing that something He did pleased us! God loves hearing about our accomplishments and appreciates when we share our worries and sadness and talk things over with Him.

I pray throughout the day but there is something about getting up near the beginning of the day with the very early morning light just beginning to show. I sit facing Crystal Peak, in the firelight and feel God's presence and peace, what a wonderful way to start the day.

On our knees together at the end of each day my husband and I thank God for his mercy and blessings. What a wonderful way to end the day.

Thank you Grace L. Naessens for giving us permission to use your magnificent poem:

The Difference
by Grace L. Naessens

I got up early one morning
and rushed right into the day;
I had so much to accomplish,
I didn't have time to pray.

Problems just tumbled about me
and grew heavier with each task;
Why doesn't God help me, I wondered;
He answered, "You didn't ask."

I wanted to see joy and beauty,
but the day toiled on, gray and bleak;
I wondered why God didn't show me
He said, "But you didn't seek."

I tried to come into God's presence;
I used all my keys at the lock;
God gently and lovingly chided,
"My child, you didn't knock."

I woke up early this morning
and paused before entering the day;
I had so much to accomplish

That I had to take time to pray.

About the authors

Candy Beebe (left) lived in Lake City for fifteen years with her husband David. They served as pastors of First Baptist Church for twelve of those years.In her words, "I often thought I should have been born in the mountains; there is a peace and assurance of God's presence and closeness at home in the San Juans."

Julie Stephens (right) lives joyfully in the mountain village of Lake City, Colorado with her husband and their dogs. She is a writer, photographer, teacher, hiker and lover of life. Her previously published books are *Reflections in the San Juan Mountains* and *Tea and Talk with Friends*, which she co-authored. Julie also pens a column for the Lake City newspaper, The Silver World, called *Life From My View*, about her perspective on living at 9,000 feet in Lake City, Colorado.

Scripture Index

Genesis 1.24-25, p191
  2.18, p45 9.14-16, p136 22.18, p40 48.9, p49
Leviticus 19.18, p106
Deuteronomy 8.10, p141
  11.18-21, p18
  29.18, p69
Joshua 4.6-7, p166
  14.11, p92
1 Kings 2.3, p144
  19.4-8, p185
Job 12.7-10, p174
Psalms 19.1, p44, p165
  27.8, p128
  27.14, p194
  32.7, p124
  37.25, p150
  46.10, p55, p129
  63.6, p171
  74.17, p124
  84, p172
  84.11, p33
  90.12, p182
  95.6, p31
  119.148, p171
  127.3, p49
  139.16, p59
  139.23-24, p170
  145.2, p68
  145.18-19, p108
  148, p175
Proverbs 4.23, p196
  10.12, p9
  13.4, p38
  17.6, p46
  17:22, p64
  18.10, p95

Proverbs 18.22, p45
  22.6, p25, p162
  24.12, p193
Ecclesiastes 2.16, p58
  3.1, p110
  3.11, p59
  7.1, p43
  7.14, p42
  12.1-7, p90
Isaiah 52.7, p151
  54.10, p104
  55.10, p76
  55.12, p44
  55.8-9, p33
  56.7, p178
Jeremiah 7.11, p178
  29.11, p7, p200
  31.33, p18
  33.6, p85
Ezekiel 36.26, p98
Daniel 1.8, p146
Joel 2.28-29, p132

Matthew 5.6, p77
  6.19-21, p60, p181
  6.34, p195
  18, p156
  18.1-5, p50
  18.5, p49
  18.6, p50 25.44-46, p21
Mark 1.35-37, p56
  8.18, p83
  10.15, p50
  11.7, p178
Luke 1.46-47, p39
  1.46-55, p39
  1.68-79, p39
  2.29-32, p42
  9.28-31, p184

Luke 11.11-13, p50
   12.15, p60
   12.32, p122
   15.7, p117
   16.10, p160
   18.18-27, p79
   18.22, p79
   19.38-40, p35
John 1.1-14, p29 4.23-24, p27 7.37-39, p130 11.6, p86 14.16-26, p71 14.6, p20
   15.5, p120
   15.22, p193
   16.7-8, p71
   16.33, p91
   17.14, p147
Acts 1.8, p156 2.1-6, p132 2.21, p122 4.12, p21 8.1, p157
Romans 1.20, p193
   1.21, p154
   3.23, p82
   6.3-4, p65
   6.13, p142
   8.31-32, p122
   12.1, p147
   12.2, p99
   12.10, p43
   15.13, p63
1 Corinthians 2.16, p99
   3.16, p179
   9.24, p199
   12.12-13, p51
   13.11-13, p26
   13.11, p31
   13.4-13, p29 13.4-8, p10
   15.53, p100
2 Corinthians 5.1, p73
   5.17, p99
Galatians 5.22-23, p112
   5.22, p8
   6.9, p140
Ephesians 1.4, p11
   2.4-6, p168
   3.16-16, p102
   5.1-2, p47
Philippians 3.20, p88
   3.21, p147
   4.4, p44
   4.6, p195
   4.6-7, p54
   4.8, p68 4.12-13, p43
1 Thessalonians 5.17, p201
1 Timothy 3.16-17, p30
   6.6-8, p68
Hebrews 8.10, p17, p99
   10.25, p173
   12.1-2, p134, p159
   12.14-15, p69
   13.8, p148
James 3.18, p61
   4.8, p32 5.18, p75
1 Peter 2.16, p193
1 John 2.1, p74, p81
   3.2, p100
   4.19, p22
3 John 2, p85
Jude 1.22, p57
Revelation 2.17, p100
   4.11, p31

Notes

The scripture quotations that are unmarked or marked (KJV) are from the Authorized King James Version.

The scripture quotations marked (NIV) are taken from the HOLY BIBLE, NEW INTERNATIONAL VERSION® NIV® Copyright©1973, 1978, 1984 by International Bible Society. Used by permission of Zondervan. All rights reserved.

The scripture quotations marked (ESV) are from The Holy Bible, English Standard Version® (ESV®), copyright © 2001 by Crossway, a publishing ministry of Good News Publishers. Used by permission. All rights reserved.

Text marked (BCP) is taken from the Book of Common Prayer 1979, released into the public domain.

All photographs, with the exception on page 46, 48 and 203 were taken by Julie Stephens.

Additional copies of **Mountain Devotional** can be obtained from handsbestrong.com

Questions or comments about this material can be directed to: support@handsbestrong.com

May the graciousness of the LORD our God be upon us; prosper the work of our hands, prosper our handiwork. Psalm 90:17

www.ingramcontent.com/pod-product-compliance
Lightning Source LLC
Chambersburg PA
CBHW062109290426
44110CB00023B/2757